# Uncoiling the Snake

# *Uncoiling*

# the Snake

**Ancient Patterns in
Contemporary Women's Lives**

*A Snake Power Reader*

*Vicki Noble, Editor*

 HarperSanFrancisco
*A Division of* HarperCollins*Publishers*

FIRST EDITION

TEXT DESIGN BY IRENE IMFELD

---

**Library of Congress Cataloging-in-Publication Data**

Noble, Vicki.

Uncoiling the snake: ancient patterns in contemporary
women's lives: a snake power reader / Vicki Noble, editor.—
1st ed.
        p.      cm.
Includes bibliographical references.
ISBN 0-06-250549-1 (alk. paper)

  1. Shamanism.  2. Goddess religion.  3. Women—Psy-
chology.  4. Feminism—Religious aspects.  I. Title.
BF1611.N63       1993
291.1'4—dc20                       91-58922
                                          CIP

---

93 94 95 96 97 ❖ RRD(H) 10 9 8 7 6 5 4 3 2

This edition is printed on acid-free paper that meets the American
National Standards Institute Z39.48 Standard.

The work of producing this volume could never have happened without the help of certain people along the way. I'd like to remember Lane Olson and Kim Larsen from *Snake Power's* early production days as a quarterly magazine. I thank the two of them for all our long and joyously inspired nights together, drinking cappuccino and designing radical, full-color pages on the Goddess and empowered women. (The original two back issues are still available! Write to *Snake Power*, 5856 College Avenue, Box 138, Oakland, CA 94618.)

Thanks to my faithful assistant, Khara Whitney-Marsh, whose help on the phone, editing articles, keeping the subscription list current, and making sense of the files has been invaluable. Thank you to Jacqueline Strauss for long hours of inputting at the computer, and to Jennifer Berezan for her help with the final editing and pulling together of this volume into its present shape. I appreciate, too, the attention from my Harper editor, Barbara Moulton, whose bright interest in the project made the transformation of *Snake Power* into a book enjoyable.

# Contents

*Introduction*    ix
    by Vicki Noble

*Two Poems: The Word Made Flesh    1
and My Malindy*
    by Joy Oshun

*The Civilization of the Goddess    9*
    by Marija Gimbutas

*The Dark Moon Phase of the Goddess    17*
    by Demetra George

*The Feminine Power of Birth    25*
    by Janet Balaskas

*Guardians of the Sacred    41*
    by Karen Vogel

*Snake Talk: Urgent Messages    49
from the Mother*
    by Naomi Newman

*Two Poems: Dreamsnake and Snakes    55*
    by Susan Hawthorne

*Overcoming the Fear of Snakes    61*
    by Wyoma

*Ancient Patterns in Present Time    65*
    by Luzclara (Machi Clarita)

**Third Stone from the Sun**     81
by Olivia Corson

**Poem: The Initiation**     91
by N. Susan McClees

**Short Story: The Manu**     95
by Bonnie Benson

**The Body of the Goddess**     99
by Rachel Pollack

**A Modern-Day Amazon**     119
by Cristina Biaggi

**Shaktism: The Goddess in India**     123
by Linda Johnsen

**Four Prayers to Shakti:**     135
**Photos and Poems**
by Gentry Görg

**Patterns of "Completion"**     145
**in Huichol Life and Art**
by Susana Valadez

**The Pattern that Connects:**     155
**Healing with Sacred Plants**
by Adele Getty

**Synchronicity and the**     167
**Shaman of Samiland**
by Gloria Feman Orenstein

# Introduction

This book is a dream come true for me, a quarterly journal transformed into a lively collection of essays, poetry, photographs, fiction, and my own free associations in regard to it all. *Snake Power: A Journal of Contemporary Female Shamanism* was a full-color statement of women's emerging power to heal. I've been a healer for fifteen years. My own personal awakening in 1976 was a classic shamanic healing crisis characterized by the universal attributes of a shamanic calling: physical illness that was becoming life threatening, visions, big dreams, a visitation, an influx of *kundalini* energy, and the power to heal in my heart and hands. Like shamans everywhere, I gave myself without reservation to the healing process, relieved to be well myself and destined to share the healing power with others. Shamans are different from doctors; they heal from their wounds, from the knowledge in their bodies and the instinctual senses that are gradually awakened through prayer, trance, and spiritual practices. The compassion and understanding born from their own suffering is the key to the art.

Female shamanic leadership—the uprising of the Dark Goddess in contemporary women—is the agenda here. The title, *Uncoiling the Snake: Ancient Patterns in Contemporary Women's Lives,* refers to the deep, hidden structure behind things and the sacred patterns to which shamans in all cultures attune themselves. The serpent is the oldest image of Goddess wisdom and healing power connected to women. From Paleolithic caves of Europe and the equally ancient rock art of Africa and Australia to the snake dreams that modern women have more and more frequently, this serpent wisdom asserts itself. Serpents are psychically sensitive and vibrationally poised to receive messages ("oracles") from the Earth Mother, and for this reason they were revered in ancient times and kept in the temples where priestesses made prophecies. This psychic sensitivity is recognized as part of women's biological birthright, being especially strong at the times of our bleeding and birthing. The menstrual shedding of the uterine skin ties women to the mystery of transformation represented by the snake, and the lunar symbolism of waxing and waning cycles points to the continuous regenerative power that is at the root of female shamanism.

In my teaching and working with women over the years, I began to notice that what was happening to us was not being articulated in the media. (Susan Faludi has documented this at length now in her incredible book, *Backlash*, pointing out that the media focused during the 1980s on "trends" that didn't exist in real women's lives while ignoring the living issues, activities, and concerns that occupied us.) Even the so-called New Age alternative magazines almost completely ignored women's concerns, causing me to pay more attention to *Elle* or *Mirabella* at the newsstand than *Yoga Journal* or *New Age*. Modern women's magazines, with their snappy coverage of current feminist issues, have become more deeply relevant to me than coverage of male spiritual teachers and their ideas. The "gender gap" is so apparent here, it begins to look like interspecies, or at least cross-cultural, communication. Except for the classic *Woman of Power*, published in Cambridge by pioneer Char McKee, in the 1980s no one seemed to want to give voice to the vital and popular thoughts of modern women experiencing radical and alternative (that is, *feminist!*) spiritual awakenings. (The new *Ms.* magazine in its present form accomplishes this beautifully, but in the late 1980s when *Snake Power* was birthed, *Ms.* was bland and liberal, carrying articles and make-up ads that differed very little from *Glamour* or *Seventeen*.)

And so, *Snake Power* was born as a response to that vacuum in publishing, and the first two issues were welcomed by women (and men) all over the country and internationally as well. Unfortunately, publishing a full-color magazine without the support of outside funding proved to be impossible. At twenty thousand dollars an issue—just for the design and printing—the project went on hold in 1990, like a caterpillar into a cocoon, awaiting rebirth. Now, thanks to the continued faith of HarperSanFrancisco (especially publisher Clayton Carlson), *Snake Power* is reincarnated into this new format, as a book of ideas and images from contemporary women of power.

All the writings in this volume are original and unpublished, with the exceptions of Marija Gimbutas's latest work and Naomi Newman's short theater piece. Some of the pieces are first-time publications for the artist and came to me as unsolicited manuscripts when *Snake Power* was active; I am thrilled to have the opportunity to give women a first chance at publicly expressing their craft. The whole concept of *Snake Power* is the spontaneous arising of a body of knowledge from women's experience that functions as a force that cannot be held back. In the same way that the Earth is releasing an energy toward survival that can be channeled and felt by us as cells in Her body, so are women's voices opening, whether we like it or not, and we find ourselves telling truths that differ from the "norms."

As editor of this volume, my interests are threefold: I am interested in classical shamanism and have selected essays that focus on contemporary women healers, their initiations, and their direct personal experiences with the healing forces. Any one of us could be called to the healing vocation at any moment in time, and these women bear witness to that living tradition functioning in an active way in our time. I also include in any work I do some attention to the ancient female-centered cultures that worshiped a Goddess, practiced peaceful coexistence, and made the most beautiful ritual art the world has ever known. Finally, I am concerned that modern women find ways of effectively channeling and housing the larger healing energies that are being released in the face of the planetary crisis in which we find ourselves today. I believe that women can act as "lightning rods" wherever they are, in whatever context they find themselves, bringing the healing power of the Goddess into our time and place. A modern medicine woman may not be a practicing, technical hands-on healer but instead might find herself organizing her neighborhood for protection of children or starting a drumming circle in her community for bringing people together in a healing way or making sure that the food served in the cafeteria at her workplace is edible rather than poisonous.

The time we are in is becoming more and more frightening to people who care about peace on earth. Women's reproductive freedom is at risk, as well as the rights of lesbians and gay people. Ancient patriarchal hordes began their invasions five thousand years ago by cutting down the sacred groves where priestesses practiced the ancient religion, and today the ancient forests are almost gone, with logging companies moving as fast as they dare to circumvent efforts at saving the trees that provide oxygen for life on earth.

One of the most terrifying specters these days is Western medicine, which has grown into a kind of mythic monster ruling this giant, chaotic kingdom that we live in. Doctors here in the United States are perceived as gods, with near-total authority over life and death; healing is believed to be effected almost totally through the use of drugs and surgery. You and I don't have the basic freedom to birth and die at home as we please or to decide what might be appropriate treatment for our cancers or to choose not to immunize our children. And the especially cruel focus of attention of these therapies on women is appalling, with (unnecessary) hysterectomies as the most frequently performed surgery and (equally unnecessary) C-sections coming in for a close second.

The cancer industry is perhaps the most active place where today's women are terrorized and oppressed with a lack of real choices. Recently I have been shocked to learn that mastectomies are routinely performed on women whose cells have been found to be only slightly abnormal (whatever that might mean), or on noninvasive cancer in the breast, even though there is no actual evidence that this type of cancer will ever turn invasive (life-threatening). We truly need to question the technology that allows these words and labels to be

*UNCOILING THE SNAKE*

given to our bodily functions by the Western medical mind. Without mammograms, it's true that lumps couldn't be found as early as they can now; on the other hand, women are intimidated into getting frequent mammograms, when the technology itself may cause cancer! And before mammograms existed, nobody would have been able to find "crystalized abnormal cells in the milk ducts" and suggest a mastectomy.

When I was nineteen years old, I gave birth to my first daughter under the guidance of a young resident in one of the country's "finest" teaching hospitals. When my daughter spit up traces of blood from the colostrum that comes before the milk flow, the resident gave me a shot to dry up my breasts and told me I couldn't nurse. The smear that he took from my breast to the laboratory had what he called abnormal cells in it. He admitted that they had no sample of women tested under such circumstances, and he didn't know if there was any need for concern. I was simply told to cease breast-feeding immediately and to shift to the bottle. Twenty years later, when I gave birth naturally to my son under the care of a midwife in Arizona, I told her this story. She informed me that blood in the colostrum is quite common, an experience that many women have, and it is of no concern. When the milk comes in the problem passes. It's something simple and biological about the milk ducts.

Women are so fearful of the threat of death by cancer that they are willing to sacrifice their breasts and uteruses, without any evidence of necessity and without first trying natural healing. If the focus here were testicles, I can assure you more options would be provided. Alternative healing, which works, is ridiculed and belittled by the health authorities, and droves of women choose the unlikely solutions of chemotherapy, radiation, and surgery to "heal" the body of its manifestation of dis-ease. In my healing circles, I have seen complete spontaneous remissions of brain tumors, endometriosis, and breast cancer. It doesn't happen every time, and I don't know how to guarantee that it will happen, but the fact that it can and does happen should surely be enough to give it a try! I have worked on clients whose blood counts were terrifyingly low, who after the work showed a significant and *measured* rise in their blood counts. I have worked on a boy in a coma who responded in demonstrable ways while he was hooked up to machines next to his bed so that even the doctor present (the boy's father) was impressed by the power of the natural healing force.

Yet I am constantly shocked to see that even women I work with in private sessions and healing circles lack the deep faith needed to effect a natural healing and repeatedly put their trust instead in the mechanized, technological approaches of Western medicine. I say this not as a judgment against individual women who are under enormous pressure to make life-and-death choices, but because I want to talk about the almost unlimited power of the medical establishment in our culture. Under the onslaught of brainwashing against so-called primitive cultures and bizarre behaviors, it is no easy task to open the mind enough to believe that drumming, chanting, and hands-on healing can be as effective, or more so, than chemicals and the surgical knife. For years women's health activists have protested that funded research on cancer and other health problems have not taken into consideration women's special needs and concerns and that the models developed for healing were entirely aimed at and related to men.

Now, in a macabre twist on the subject, a new drug for preventing cancer is being tested on a large group of American women who will be chosen as guinea pigs based on their predisposition to cancer (by heredity) or their age range, and it is being touted as a response to this criticism that women's needs were being ignored. But no such group of men has ever been asked to experimentally ingest a chemical that may turn out to have side effects undreamed of at the present time. Only women's bodies are used in this offhanded way. So what is not new at all is being marketed as a brand new, and even feminist, solution. This is precisely the way backlash works, and it is devastating to see how effective it is. I believe we are in danger

*UNCOILING THE SNAKE*

of falling into a state of mass hypnosis from which we will not awaken and because of which our entire species will become extinct.

*Uncoiling the Snake* is an effort to present material that comes from another perspective, a radical female sensibility that puts its faith in the body, Nature, and the instincts. Some of the pieces poke fun at established ways of thinking and being; others launch a direct and serious assault on the dominant system. I have chosen the pieces presented in this volume not because I completely agree with each woman's approach, but because I think they are thoughtful and provocative and speak with integrity to the very complex issues we face at the end of the twentieth century. The potency that emerges when the serpent uncoils herself and rises is creative, providing the means for making a new world from the dying embers of the old. As the systems around us break down and disintegrate, it is important and urgent that we recognize and use the new energy flowing through us. This creative energy is part of the heat that heals, and I hope you feel it channeling through the offerings in this book.

*Vicki Noble. Summer Solstice 1992. Blessed Be.*

*Joy Oshun*

# Two Poems

Uncoiling the Snake *opens with two poems from Joy Oshun, who says about herself that she values physical health and well-being, ritual circling with women, writing, and teaching. She can be found at the Pima Community College Writing Department in Tucson, Arizona. "The Word Made Flesh" evokes the ancient African heritage of humanity as well as gives voice to the organic, instinctual process of female creativity. As something from deep within the psyche struggles to release itself into the open, a woman gets free. "My Malindy" is a singing affirmation of the woman freed into her own voice.*

## *The Word Made Flesh*

"Jump at de sun"[1]
—Words of a mother to a daughter named Zora

Lightning flashes
again and again
many times again
and my eyes open
to a new world.

Here I have no family,
no children, no friends,
no lovers. No one expects me.
Nothing here but Nakedness. The Desert.
And Time. And that something
that wants to remember.
I am not an old woman yet
Nor am I young.
My childhood and youth are gone
Part of another life
But my body wants to remember
My blood wants to remember
My heart wants to remember
who and what it took to get me here
and where I've been.
I stare at my breasts, my belly,
my hands in my lap, my legs, my feet.
The earth trembles
Have I moved?
Or is it just my remembering
drumming down my bones?


The stones moan, and I drop
to my knees suddenly, my hands
wanting to touch them, to bless them,
for they are as old as eternity

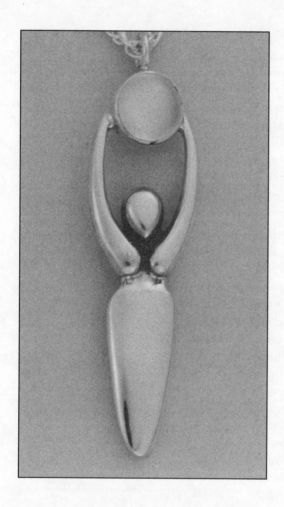

*Fig. 1. Raised*
*Arm Goddess*
*Holding Moon*
*© Jane Iris*
*Designs, Inc.*

They are the Oracles of Time
They are the Spirits of the Ancestors
They are the voice of The Mother
They carry the burdens of the earth,
of humankind, and my own heart
They know my story and what it took
to get me here, to this place of
Spirit Voices. And Magic.

*A SNAKE POWER READER*

The desert floor begins to hum
The chaparral secretes its fragrance
The Night-Blooming Cereus opens before my eyes
Something taps softly but insistently at my breastbone
I rise on my haunches, wait, and listen,
my black skin glistening silver in moonlight
and through the silver whispering,
> "Find the heart within the stone
> and set us free and set us free
> Remember your name and who you are
> and we will set you free."

My hands fall to the ground
I strain to push it out then
To remember my name
To remember my name
In my soul there's a soft explosion
My ears pop. And I hear mountains
resounding my name, the mission bells
in the distance chiming my name,
the wings of the desert moth
sputtering my name,
the doves in the mesquite trees
murmuring my name
affirming my name
I raise my hands to the heavens
crying out my name:
> Jemima. Jemima. Jemima.[2]
> Jemima is my name.
> I take back my name
> I praise my name
> I cherish my name
> I honor my name
> Jemima. Jemima. Jemima.

Into the dawn I chant my name, I sing my name
Jemima. Jemima. Jemima.

*UNCOILING THE SNAKE*

The sun rises, radiant and worshipful,
as I. For I have reclaimed my name
and know why I am here:

> My belly is swollen with stories
> My breasts hang heavy with stories
> My neck distends with stories
> My eyes bulge with stories
> My teeth throb with stories
> My vulva quickens with stories
> My leg muscles cramp with stories
> My back muscles scream with stories
> My heart quakes with stories
> My pores flush with stories
> My bones groan with stories
> My brain cells swirl with stories
> My nerves bristle with stories
> My skin prickles with stories
> My blood rumbles with stories
> My soul surges with stories
> My fingers are stiff with stories
> My tongue is seized with stories

I am here because I am alive
and heavy with fertility
Keeping company with the Stones, and Magic,
and this body full of stories.

© *May 1990*

**Notes**

1. Zora Neale Hurston, "My Folks," *Dust Tracks on a Road: An Autobiography,*
   ed. Robert Hemenway (Chicago: University of Illinois Press, 1984), p. 21.
2. Jemima is a name fraught with negative racial overtones now associated
   with Black Woman. But Jemima, Yemimah, is a Jewish name meaning
   dove.

## *My Malindy*

She's sleeping now, my Malindy
I stroke her dreds
wild, smelling of clay
and coconut
                        Openmouthed
she breathes unevenly
through the gap between her teeth

Many years ago
I learned that my anger
and rage over my pain
was not acceptable: I was bad
or talking back or uncouth
Then I grew up
into a proud hussy
Now I was
                        unreasonable
                crazy
            demanding
        stubborn
        or a Bitch
when I spoke up

In time she became a monster
finally a demon
                        So I banished her
into the recesses
of my being
—the place of the bogeyman
Somewhere she could
holler all she wanted
and I wouldn't hear her

Then I became a Lady
Smiling
Respectable

*Fig. 2. African
Fertility Goddess
© Jane Iris
Designs, Inc.*

No hint of a spook
                    One day
someone I loved
tried to erase my existence

When I came out of the whirlwind
I could hear

        Malindy screaming

    Ravaged
      Uncaged
        Outraged
at my grievous and unconscionable act
I had put her away

        Out of my life
        Out of my thoughts
        Out of my feelings and actions

I am not a Lady anymore
In my eyes you will see the Amazon
should you seek to violate me
in your desperation and your pain

And when my Malindy sings

        Passionate
        Strident
        Discordant
So I do — Until what needs be done
Listening to her I create peace
Listening to her I become a warrior of peace

She's sleeping now, my Malindy
At home. At last. And loved.

© *January 1991*

**UNCOILING THE SNAKE**

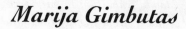

*Marija Gimbutas*

# The Civilization of the Goddess

*By this time, most readers of this work have heard the name of Marija Gimbutas, the archaeologist who fled Lithuania during Hitler's onslaught with a baby under one arm and a dissertation in the other. She ended up at Harvard University in an unpaid position for several years, not even allowed to eat in the all-men's dining room! Finally, she received a tenured position at UCLA, where she taught until she retired a few years ago.*

*Always independent, born of two doctors who raised her with a sense of belonging and self-esteem, Marija did not set out to become a feminist archaeologist. But her scientific scrutiny led to radical findings, and her need to tell the truth made her a maverick in her field. Today she is the preeminent*

9

*authority on ancient Goddess civilizations in Old Europe, having documented their millennial presence, the overthrowing of these cultures, and the bloody transition to patriarchy brought on by the invasion of the Indo-Europeans five thousand years ago.*

*The living presence of the ancient Goddess archetype is elaborated in Marija's themes and content and, even more impressively, is embodied in her life. It is an honor to be able to share a little of the writing from her latest voluminous work,* The Civilization of the Goddess.

According to myriad images that have survived from the great span of human prehistory on the Eurasian continents, it was the sovereign mystery and creative power of the female as the source of life that developed into the earliest religious experiences. The Great Mother Goddess who gives birth to all creation out of the holy darkness of her womb became a metaphor for Nature herself, the cosmic giver and taker of life, ever able to renew Herself within the eternal cycle of life, death, and rebirth.

Flint sculptures of female figures and animals have been found that date as far back as the Acheulian period of the Lower Paleolithic, more than 500,000 years ago.[1] From the Middle Paleolithic-Mousterian epoch, 100,000 to 40,000 years ago, triangular stones were deliberately placed above burials and cupmarks were engraved into stones. This very early religious symbolism has yet to be systematically studied; most research has been done on the Upper Paleolithic period, 40,000 to 10,000 years before our present time.

A veritable explosion of art took place during the Upper Paleolithic, expressed by innumerable cave paintings, rock carvings, and sculptures. The caves in which we find exquisite animal drawings and engravings were sanctuaries for the enactment of seasonal rites, initiation rituals, and other ceremonies related to a participation in the sacred cycles of life.[2] Miniature sculptures in stone, horn, or bone, representing a variety of deities, appeared between 27,000 and 25,000 B.C.E. About three thousand sculptures have been found in the area between southern France and central Siberia.[3] From such an abundant sample, we may approximate their figurative significance. The various shapes, gestures, and attributes portrayed on these sculptures, in addition to their provenance, lend themselves to a classification of types representing various aspects and functions of the Goddess.

The very earliest symbols engraved on rocks and articles of bone or horn reflect a profound belief in a life-generating Goddess who represents One Source while pictured in many forms. From as early as 25,000 B.C.E., she is depicted with exaggerated breasts, vulva, and buttocks, indicating the centers of emanation of her procreative powers. A study of symbols in Paleolithic art demonstrates that the female, rather than the male, was the deity of creation. In fact, there are no traces in Paleolithic art of a father figure. The bearing and nourishing of offspring—plant, animal, and human—was the primary model for the development of the image of the Goddess as the all-generating deity.

Miniature sculptures of female figures carved from ivory or soft stone were not "Venuses," as they tend to be identified in literature, nor were they "fertility charms" designed to arouse male sexuality. Their functions were considerably more important: the giving and protection of life, as well as death and regeneration. The Goddess personifies the eternally renewing cycle of life in all of its forms and manifestations. An interpretation of these functions follows from careful study of particular attributes of these early sculptures: their postures, gestures, headgear, and associated religious symbols. Numerous expressions of the divine female, which persisted for many thousands of years, can be clearly seen from extant artifacts from the Upper Paleolithic.

We find at this time an iconography of the Goddess comprised of several kinds of abstract or hieroglyphic symbols: X's, V's, triangles, meanders, and the like; representational images such as vulvae, breasts, and birds' feet; and animal symbols representing various aspects of the Goddess, embodying her power. Essentially the same iconography attended the religion of the Goddess well into the agricultural era, although evolved, reflecting changing economic conditions.

During the Neolithic there was a renewed flowering of artistic expression. The invention of ceramics, c. 6500 B.C.E., marked the appearance of thousands of figurines and vases,

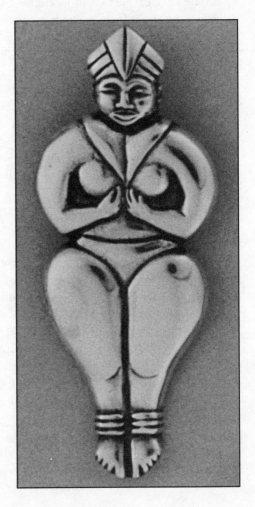

*Fig. 3. Ishtar Image*
*© Jane Iris Designs, Inc.*

temples and their miniature models, wall paintings, reliefs, and countless ritual articles. The number of religious symbols multiplied a hundredfold, providing abundant data for deciphering the Goddess's iconography. Moreover, the symbolism of Old Europe, 6500–3500 B.C.E., provides an essential key to understanding Paleolithic religion, since many of the images are continuous. The reconstruction of this symbolic system is described by this author in *The Language of the Goddess*.[4]

The figurines represent various images of the Goddess, portrayed articulately with details of attire and headdress or reduced to bare outlines. The latter, very likely, were *ex votos*, or amulets in her image. Figurines have been recovered in temples on altars, on oven platforms, in specially prepared offering places, and in caves and graves. They have frequently been found in caches stored in vases, or as miniature tableaux representing certain religious activities. Obviously, groups of figurines were used for the reenactment of rituals. The incessant production of figurines witnesses an energetic process shared by all participants.

There are at least twenty female and five male anthropomorphic and half-human, half-animal figurine types that differ in posture, facial features, masks, headgear, and associated symbols. These identifiable images are also portrayed in reliefs and paintings on temple or cave walls and on vases.

The multiple categories, functions, and symbols used by prehistoric peoples to express the Great Mystery are all aspects of the unbroken unity of one deity, a Goddess who is ultimately Nature herself.
*(excerpted from pp. 222–23)*

There is no doubt that the prehistoric veneration of Mother Earth survived intact up to the time of the worship of Demeter and Persephone in Greece, Ops Consiua in Rome, Nerthus in Germanic lands, Zemyna or Zemes Mate in the Baltic area, Mother Moist Earth in Slavic lands, and elsewhere. Her power was too ancient and deep to be altogether destroyed by succeeding patriarchal religions, including

Christianity. She was therefore absorbed, and became known in western Europe as various saints: Radegund, Macrine, Walpurga, Milburga, among others.[5] In many other lands, especially eastern Europe, she fused with the Mother of God, Marija.

The Black Madonna is this same Earth Mother, whose blackness represents the color of earth's fertility. The yearly renewal of her fecundity is her fundamental miracle. Ancient mysteries, enacted throughout prehistoric and historic millennia—in caves, cemeteries, temples, and in the open fields—were for the purpose of expressing gratitude to the source of all life and nourishment, and to ritually participate in the secret of the earth's abundance.
*(excerpted from p. 230)*

The earliest civilizations of the world—in China, Tibet, Egypt, the Near East, and Europe—were, in all probability, matristic "Goddess civilizations." Since agriculture was developed by women, the Neolithic period created optimum conditions for the survival of matrilineal, endogamous systems inherited from Paleolithic times. During the early agricultural period women reached the apex of their influence in farming, arts and crafts, and social functions. The matriclan with collectivist principles continued.

There is no evidence in all of Old Europe of a patriarchal chieftainate of the Indo-European type. There are no male royal tombs and no residences in megarons on hill forts. The burial rites and settlement patterns reflect a matrilineal structure, whereas the distribution of wealth in graves speaks for an economic egalitarianism.

. . .

A serious and continuous obstacle in the study of ancient societies is the indolent assumption that they must have resembled our own. Bachofen warned in 1859 that "the scholar must be able to renounce the ideas of his own time and transfer himself to the midpoint of a completely different world of thought,"[6]

*UNCOILING THE SNAKE*

but the existence of "a different world" is the hardest thing to admit. The difficulty with the term *matriarchy* in twentieth century anthropological scholarship is that it is assumed to represent a complete mirror image of patriarchy or andro-cracy—that is to say, a hierarchical structure with women rul-ing by force in the place of men. This is far from the reality of Old Europe. Indeed, we do not find in Old Europe, nor in all of the Old World, a system of autocratic rule by women with an equivalent suppression of men. Rather, we find a structure in which the sexes are more or less on an equal footing, a society that could be termed a *gylany*. This is a term coined by Riane Eisler (from *gyne*, referring to woman, and *andros*, man, linked by the letter *l* for *lyein*, to resolve, or *lyo*, to set free). Gylany implies that the sexes are "linked" rather than hierar-chically "ranked."[7] I use the term *matristic* simply to avoid the term *matriarchy*, with the understanding that it incorporates matriliny.

*(excerpted from p. 324)*

## Notes

1. Lithic sculptures and symbolic marks are present from the Achecullean and Mousterian periods; see J. E. Musch, "Animal Farm Paleolithic Sculptures from the Northwest European Plains" (paper presented at the World Archaeology Congress, Southhampton, 1986). Also *"Bilderbuch der Steinzeit." Archäologische Berichten* 20 (1991).
2. See the splendid book on Upper Paleolithic caves and sanctuaries and their art: A. Leroi-Gourhan, *Treasures of Prehistoric Art* (New York: Harry N. Abrams, 1967).
3. H. Delporte, *L'image de la femme dans l'art préhistorique* (Paris: Picard, 1979).
4. Marija Gimbutas, *The Language of the Goddess: Unearthing the Hidden Symbols of Western Civilization* (San Francisco: Harper & Row, 1989).
5. Pamela Berger, *The Goddess Obscured: Transformation of the Grain Protectress from Goddess to Saint* (Boston: Beacon Press, 1985): pp. 49–70.
6. J. J. Bachofen, *Myth, Religion and Mother Right: Selected Writings*, trans. Ralph Manheim (Bollinger: Princeton University Press, 1973), series 84, p. 81.
7. Riane Eisler, *The Chalice and the Blade* (San Francisco: Harper & Row, 1987).

*Demetra George*

# The
# Dark Moon Phase
# of the Goddess

*Marija Gimbutas's work has catalyzed women to think about our ancient past in a variety of ways. In the following piece, astrologer Demetra George speculates on how an eightfold lunar phase cycle might overlay on human cultural evolution from Paleolithic times, through the flowering of the Goddess in the Neolithic period, into our present nightmare of patriarchal violence and male domination. Demetra's provocative suggestion that the Goddess herself, for her own renewal and regeneration, chose to go underground for five thousand years, has sparked a lively debate in audiences around the country. Demetra and I carry on a fairly continuous dialogue ourselves about whether the last five thousand years are a terrible mistake that needs fixing or an organic cycle that's*

*coming to a natural conclusion! Either way, I think you'll enjoy her musings. For a more thorough development of her arguments, see her new book,* Mysteries of the Dark Moon: The Healing Power of the Dark Goddess *(San Francisco: Harper-SanFrancisco, 1992).*

With the "Return of the Goddess," researchers in the fields of art history, mythology, archaeology, and theology are uncovering evidence of a flowering of matriarchal culture thousands of years ago and its subsequent demise beginning in the fourth millennium B.C.E. Many feminist scholars have shown that the ancient societies that worshiped the earth and moon as Goddess were the victims of centuries of continual persecutions and were intentionally destroyed by violent patriarchal tribes who followed the solar and sky gods.

In my latest work, *Mysteries of the Dark Moon,* I question this limited analysis and suggest that the disappearance of the Goddess and women of power during the last five-thousand-year patriarchal period was a factor built into her own cosmology of cyclic renewal, as mirrored in the waxing and waning phases of the moon's cycle. The Goddess is essentially a personification of the continually self-renewing energy symbolized in the lunar cycle and celebrated in the Wheel of the Year. In the same way that the moon cycles from new to full to dark and back again to new, the Goddess herself has cycles of birth, growth, death, and renewal that transpire over generations of time in the cultural evolution of humanity.

If the Goddess is true to her own essential nature, she will resonate in attunement to the moon's rhythms of ebb and flow and, like the moon, will periodically withdraw into the dark phase of her cycle. Here she performs her mysteries of renewal. If we look closely at the rhythm of the moon's cycle, we may perceive that the development and flowering of the

Goddess, her subsequent disappearance, and her current reemergence may be due to her natural cycle of waxing and waning phases.

The new, full, and dark phases of the moon are a metaphor for the beginnings, middles, and endings of all our life endeavors. Comparing the moon's cycle to the growth of a plant, life begins at the new moon with the birth of something new. A seed germinates and sends forth its first tender shoots above the ground. The waxing part of the cycle consists of building some kind of form that can contain this impulse, dream, or sense of purpose. The full moon stage of cyclic process is analogous to the flowering and fruiting of the seed. It is a time to accomplish our intention and to live out the meaning and purpose of our aspiration. The waning part of the moon's cycle can be likened to the harvest; then fruit that has been left on the vine to go to seed decomposes. We reap the benefits of our crop, then let go of a form that has fulfilled its purpose and depleted its store of vital energy. The essence of the wisdom that we have gained from the process becomes the kernel for the new seed that is buried underground, awaiting germination with the initiation of the next cycle.

Let us look at the historical rise and fall of the Goddess culture and religion and see if we can discover any correspondences between the life cycle of an evolving feminine principle embodied in the Goddess and the symbolic meaning of the successive phases of the moon's cycle. We know that the Goddess culture began to decline around 3000 B.C.E. Our much later fairy tales tell us that Snow White and Sleeping Beauty were poisoned by the Wicked Stepmother and Bad Fairy (the Dark Goddess) and then fell into long swoons encased in a deathlike sleep. These stories carry the mythic image of the Goddess and the feminine, who also have been in a deep slumber. The mythological tales repeatedly tell us of the Moon Goddesses who periodically disappeared to bathe in the sacred springs in order to renew their virginity and be born anew. We now see, as we approach the year 2000 C.E., that the Goddess is definitely reborn, as evidenced in the current proliferation of her circles, stories, chants, images, and rituals.

The feminine energies virtually disappeared from Western culture for about five thousand years. If we place this period of dormancy within the context of the lunation cycle, this corresponds to a five-thousand-year (3000 B.C.E.–2000 C.E.) dark phase of a historical cycle. If the dark balsamic phase comprises one-eighth of the lunation cycle, then the entire previous lunar life cycle that relates to the Goddess must be eight-times-five thousand or forty thousand years in duration. If this is the case, then we can propose that at about 38,000 B.C.E. a new vision and aspiration of the feminine principle was birthed and released at the beginning new moon phase of one of her life cycles.

This time, the dawn of the Upper Paleolithic, around 38,000 B.C.E., corresponds to a momentous turning point in our evolution—the first appearance of *Homo sapiens* in western Europe, from whom all present-day humanity is descended. Anatomically modern people with vastly enhanced intellectual powers arrived, probably from Africa, carrying new tools. They made rapid advances in the technology of survival and quickly replaced the previous inhabitants, the Neanderthal. These new people had the capacity for symbolic thinking and demonstrated a skill in creating images. This ability blossomed into astonishing artistic accomplishments. In an area spanning Eurasia from Spain to Siberia, archaeologists have unearthed thousands of carved, engraved, and sculpted images that emphasized the breasts, belly, buttocks, and vulva of the generous, lush female body.

The archaeological evidence indicates that the people who suddenly emerged at the beginning of the Upper Paleolithic displayed a reverence for the feminine. According to our model of the Goddess's lunar cycle, at the beginning of the Upper Paleolithic the evolving feminine principle gave birth to a vision that would unfold over the course of her forty-

thousand-year life cycle. The kernel of this seed was a reverence for the mystery of the life-giving powers of the universe
and an intention to decipher the secrets of how it is that life is
created, sustained, and regenerated.

For the prehistoric peoples, the ability to secure a stable
food supply determined whether or not life could survive. And
so part of the quest of the evolving feminine principle was
the search for the means by which to keep the life force alive
and continuous. The female body contained the secret to producing food for the infant child; what key would unlock the
mystery of the earth's body to produce the same relatively predictable secure source of food in order to sustain her adult
human children? The technological advances in the first half of
the Upper Paleolithic were focused on inventing and refining

*Fig. 4. Mother
Goddess
© Jane Iris
Designs, Inc.*

**A SNAKE POWER READER**

tools to better hunt, skin, and prepare the animals, their primary food source.

The fruition phase of the Goddess's lunar life cycle occurred around 11,000 B.C.E. At this time, it has been shown that women discovered the seed of agriculture and the invention of cooking, transforming the seed to grain and then into bread. The discovery of agriculture—that a seed can be planted, cultivated, and harvested—is the fruit of the vision that was germinated at the beginning of the Upper Paleolithic. Twenty-eight thousand years after the evolving feminine principle initiated a new cycle of growth, *Homo sapiens's* reverence for the birth-giving and life-sustaining powers of the Great Goddess yielded the secret of a stable and predictable food source from the body of the Earth Mother herself. The capacity to produce food rather than to simply hunt and gather it was the apex of the Goddess's cycle.

This achievement led to the harvest period of the Goddess's lunar life cycle during the Neolithic era, one in which civilization could be created. With the development of agriculture, a more settled life and stable food supply provided people with the leisure time to engage in other activities— religion, politics, trade, science, and the arts. In the ruins of the earliest Neolithic settlements such as Jericho (9500 B.C.E.), Catal Hüyük (6500 B.C.E.), Halicar (5600 B.C.E.), and southeastern Europe (7000 B.C.E.) are found numerous testimonies to the worship of the Goddess that inspired a tremendous outpouring of creative arts and social progress.

A seed vision of the feminine principle as the source, sustainer, and regenerator of life, released at the new moon phase in the beginning of the Upper Paleolithic, now by the last quarter harvest phase of the Neolithic had developed into prosperous, peaceful, and highly refined civilizations. The Neolithic cultures held a complex set of religious beliefs timed to the seasonal agricultural celebration that venerated the Triple Goddess and her horned and hoofed consort as cocreators in the mystery of life.

All of this began to change around 3000 B.C.E., which demarcates the transition between the demise of the goddesses and the rise of the gods. This is when the patriarchal nomads first invaded the lands of the Neolithic Goddess. This time period corresponds with the dark balsamic (closure) phase of the Goddess's lunar life cycle.

Many recent books chronicle the events leading to the eventual abolition and death of the Goddess, the suppression of women, and the devaluation of Nature and the feminine. Many of these works tell what happened, but the question of why it happened is rarely or only superficially addressed. Why, in the third millennium B.C.E., did the feminine principle decrease as the predominant governing force in religion and society? Was the nature of the peoples who followed the solar gods inherently violent, destructive, and ruthless against the worshipers of the moon goddesses? Or might there exist larger forces operating on cosmic levels that can give a broad perspective to the monumental changes that transformed the face of the earth at this time?

In this analysis, the destruction of the Goddess culture occurred within a context of the dark phase of a large-scale cosmic cycle. The decline of the Goddess may have been a natural factor of the decreasing and withdrawing energies that are an inherent aspect of the dark moon phase of cyclic process. During the closure phase of a forty-thousand-year cycle, the evolving feminine principle embodied in the Goddess entered into a deep incubatory sleep. She had accomplished her intention for *Homo sapiens* to discover the secrets of creating and sustaining, which led to the discovery of agriculture and the creation of civilization. Having exhausted her supply of vital energy, she retreated into her dark recessive phase in order to actualize her third great mystery, that of regeneration.

*Janet Balaskas*

# The
# Feminine
# Power of Birth

Kundalini, *as it is called in India, refers to a latent energy coiled like a snake at the base of the spine. It is the source of spontaneously arising heat that heals and empowers, and it belongs naturally to women through our biological processes of bleeding and birthing.* Kundalini *is the foundation for our strength, courage, psychic power, and creativity. The practices that would naturally lead to its arousal and development have been largely preempted by men in the twentieth-century Western world, leaving modern women with a helpless, empty feeling of victimization. We need to be giving birth naturally at home under the skillful hands of midwives, as was our practice until the Middle Ages in Europe when the witch craze killed almost all the women healers or drove them*

*underground. And we need to be free to explore and manifest our artistic creativity in a vital and dynamic way, without some rigid, male-dominated art establishment passing judgment on our expression. The following pieces speak to these two essential female expressions, birthing and creativity.*

*Janet Balaskas is the founder of the Active Birth movement and director of the International Active Birth Centre in London. She is the mother of four children and author of seven books. Her heartfelt activism shines through this article as well as in her highly acclaimed book,* Active Birth *(Boston: Harvard Common Press, 1992). Her other titles, audio cassettes, and videos are available by mail order from the Active Birth Centre, 55 Dartmouth Park Road, London NW5 1SL.*

W oman, as her name implies, is the human with a womb. Her body is miraculous. Throughout the vulnerable months of pregnancy, she shelters the unborn child and has the power to give birth and to nurture new human life. In matriarchal cultures all over the world, the procreative power of women was honored. Sacred images of the pregnant and birthing Goddess are found in every ancient culture going back as far as Paleolithic times. Woman's biological rhythms gave meaning to cultural and social life.

For example, menstruation signified a time of power, a monthly flowering of the womb, and a renewal of fertility, which usually occurred synchronistically among women living together and coincided with the rising of the full moon. In matristic tribal societies, both ancient and modern, pregnancy is a normal part of everyday life. The pregnant mother continues with her daily work throughout this period of incubation, dignified and beautiful, filled with the vital energy of her unborn child. She is advised by her female elders to increase her activity and gather her strength for the birth, calculated to occur around the tenth full moon after the child was conceived.[1]

By contrast, in our modern world, where peace teeters on a knife edge, fashion honors the slender, boyish figure. Menstruation is seen as a curse, a time of weakness, a messy inconvenience to the modern woman. She has no time to respect the rhythmic cycles of her own biology or to have any sense of their relationship to the seasonal and planetary cycles. Pregnancy is usually seen as a time of weakness and indisposition. Social ritual and care surrounding the pregnant mother emphasize the routine search for pathology in medical clinics. The white-coated doctor is God. The peering eye of the ultrasound scanner (originally invented to detect submarines) and the probing needle of the amniocentesis invade the mystery and the privacy of the womb. The medical mind penetrates deep into the body of woman, assessing, diagnosing, and predicting the unpredictable.

Throughout pregnancy, the woman's trust and confidence in her body are ritually undermined. She loses her connection with nature's miraculous forces of creation, which are inherent within her body, and the power of her intuition and instincts are cast aside as irrational, trivial, or unreliable. Her lifestyle generally minimizes physical activity in pregnancy, which when combined with a mental surrender of faith in her power to the medical establishment increases the chances of a long or difficult labor.

Despite all the rigorous antenatal "care" offered to our mothers, there has never been a civilization on earth in which women have experienced such difficulty and so much complication in birthing. This is one of the most obvious symptoms of the dis-ease of our times. Without exaggeration, modern childbirth can be called, in the words of psychiatrist R. D. Laing, "a disaster zone of human experience." The domination and suppression of the feminine is at its most brutal and mechanistic when a woman in childbirth, without any justifying complications, lies on her back and opens her legs on an obstetric table. She is powerless and helpless, defying the physiological logic of her body and entirely at the mercy of her (usually) male doctor, who has the privilege of extracting her baby. It is time for all women to see that the difficulties modern women have in childbirth are "iatrogenic" (caused by doctors).*

Undoubtedly, obstetric interventions such as the modern cesarean are marvelous when used appropriately to serve rather than to control mothers and their babies. Every modern woman can be reassured by the availability of obstetric backup when there are difficulties, complications, or in an emergency. I also do not include in my criticisms the small percentage of "feminist" obstetricians, both male and female, who have faith in women's ability to give birth naturally—and know how to stand back, ready to help only when necessary. However, the fact is that obstetricians are the ambulance men. It is time for them to step back and relinquish control over normal childbirth and to recognize that they are failing dismally to improve upon nature.

If we survey the state of affairs in the great industrialized nations of the world, where birth has been replaced by obstetrics, we are in for a shock. Here are a few well-known general statistics: In parts of the United States and Canada as many as 50 percent of babies are born by cesarean section, with a national average of 25 percent (one in four). This reflects a 400 percent increase in twenty years.[2] In parts of Brazil and southern Italy, the percentage of cesarean sections can be as high as 90 percent. In Greece around 70 percent of the births are chemically induced. Even in Great Britain, where we pride ourselves on being a pioneering nation in the move toward natural childbirth, we have the highest intervention rate in Europe, and about 85 percent of our first-time mothers are given some form of interventive help to give birth. Only 1 percent of British mothers give birth in their own homes, where condi-

*Editor's note: I believe the word *iatrogenic,* meaning "doctor-caused," was first used by the social critic Ivan Illich in his brilliant work, *Medical Nemesis,* in which he criticizes Western medicine for disempowering people and causing more problems than it solves.

tions are most conducive to physiological childbirth. By contrast, Holland has 35 percent of home births and the best birth statistics of any industrialized nation.[3]

Professor G. J. Kloosterman, the famous "feminist" obstetrician from Amsterdam, Holland, has said:

> If they could prove in the United States that their results in birth were better than ours, then we would have to change to the American system. I must confess personally that I do not believe that technology will ever improve on natural labor in a healthy woman. . . . On the other hand, we are trying to investigate whether too much monitoring in normal labor will in fact detract from normality and do harm. I am convinced that for human beings, as for other animals, labor goes best if the woman feels completely at ease.[4]

Many modern women are told by their doctors that electronic monitoring of their babies during labor enhances safety and that is why they are wise to give birth in a hospital, where such equipment is readily available. *In fact, these monitors restrict the woman's normal mobility and create the very conditions most likely to induce fetal distress (shortage of oxygen), which they are supposed to prevent.* When a woman has what I call an Active Birth, she moves instinctively and naturally adopts positions that insure good circulation of blood to the womb and good fetal oxygenation. Her body knows what is best for her baby.

Recently, studies from different parts of the world have shown conclusively that Kloosterman's suspicions are right: routine electronic fetal heart monitoring in labor results in an increase in the rate of cesareans, rather than the desired result of cesarean prevention.[5] This leads visionaries such as Michael Odent to say that the electronic era in childbirth is over. This is becoming more and more obvious in the West, but regrettably the influence of our example has already spread far and wide throughout the world.

Tragically, even in the developing countries, where traditional childbirth practices have continued until fairly recently, it is difficult to find a local midwife nowadays who is still attending births, except in rural areas. Most of the women who have access to a modern hospital are hurrying to follow the high-tech example. And yet, evidence of numerous studies tells us that childbirth in tribal societies the world over was usually uncomplicated and seemingly much shorter and easier for our primitive sisters than it is for modern mothers.[6]

Obstetrics is a relatively recent phenomenon. Legend has it that approximately three hundred years ago in the seventeenth century, Louis the XIV required his mistress, Madame de Montespan, to give birth on her back so he could have a good view of the proceedings. In 1738 the obstetrician to the Queen of France, Francois Mauriceau, introduced among the French aristocracy the idea (gleaned from Aristotle) that women should give birth on their backs in bed. He said that it was easier because it saved having to put them to bed afterward! In the midseventeenth century forceps were invented by the British-born Chamberlen brothers. These forceps deliveries were carried out secretively under black drapes. Astonishingly, even without anesthesia, they became popular among women of fashion.

Midwives were replaced by physicians, surgeons descended from barbers, and womanly wisdom was taken over by the masculine control of an increasingly patriarchal society. As the industrial age became more firmly entrenched, more women, led by the aristocracy, lay flat on their backs during labor and birth in a position of helplessness for the convenience of their doctors. Midwives were regarded as witches and some of them were rumored to have been burned at the stake.*

*Editor's note: Feminist research has documented the shocking methods and numbers of Inquisition murders of midwives and healers during the Middle Ages in Europe. For information, see B. Ehrenreich and D. English, Witches, Midwives and Nurses: A History of Women Healers (New York: Glass Mountain Pamphlets, 1972) and Complaints and Disorders: The Sexual Politics of Sickness (New York: Glass Mountain/Feminist Press, 1973).

By the end of the eighteenth century, birth stools had disappeared. Birth had become a medical event. The art of midwifery became the science of obstetrics. This movement reached a peak with the invention of anesthesia around the beginning of this century. Queen Victoria in England was one of the first women to take chloroform while giving birth. Since then, obstetrics has become more and more sophisticated and more deeply entrenched.[7]

I believe it is vital for the healing of our planet that women the world over—whether directly involved in a pregnancy or not—can clearly see and understand the degradation of the feminine that has taken place and is still taking place all around us for pregnant and birthing mothers. Childbirth is a deeply feminist issue, to be taken up by all of us, especially those who are currently not engaged in childbearing and not therefore influenced by the hormonal secretions that turn our awareness and power inward, making us vulnerable and unready for political battle in the world. Let's look at a typical birth scene from the twentieth century from an American textbook used by obstetrics nurses. This is the sort of book that falls into medical libraries all over the world and influences students during their training.[8] The words *obstetric nurse* already define her role as handmaiden to the obstetrician, who is really in control of childbirth. The midwife (with the woman) has almost totally lost her professional autonomy in the United States.

The photographs in this book of a so-called normal birth are the sort of images of birth most modern women have grown up with and are conditioned to expect. The mother is draped with sheets, lying flat on her back, with only her genital area showing. You see a little square, known as the "sterile field." Isolated as if for operation, with all her pubic hair shaved off, the genital area is rudely exposed for all to see and swabbed with antiseptics. The mandatory episiotomy makes it look as if the baby is born from a wound. The poor mother struggles to lift her head to see what is going on at the other end of her body from which she is more or less detached.

*Fig. 5. Birth Rite, by Betty LaDuke. Editor's note: I chose these images by Betty LaDuke because I have always loved them and because, like almost no other birthing images I've seen, they illustrate the way in which birth is not only sacred but shamanic. When a woman gives birth naturally, she is in an altered state while remaining physically present and aware. She stands at the doorway between life and death, facing the unknown, and with the help of the elemental forces and the animal allies, she brings a new soul from the invisible realm of the spirit into our world. This is quintessentially shamanic and is the prototype for all initiation practices around the world.*

*UNCOILING THE SNAKE*

*Fig. 6. Rites of Passage, by Betty LaDuke.*

Not so long ago obstetric stirrups were used for normal birth. In too many places this practice still exists. With her feet in stirrups, the mother is not only helpless and powerless, but utterly humiliated and degraded. She is completely at the mercy of those around her, who are total strangers, with her most tender and vulnerable parts open to invasion; often she is

*A SNAKE POWER READER*

drugged or unconscious as well. Belief in the myth that this
model is safest causes millions of women and midwives still to
collude with it. A few improvements are added, such as new
decor to the birth room in a hospital or flowery wallpaper. Expensive adjustable birthing beds on first appearance look as if
they are designed for a country cottage, but they convert at the
flick of a switch into a full obstetric delivery table. These may
be attempts to acknowledge the environmental needs of
women for a homelike environment or a more upright posture,
but they are cosmetic tokens of what is really needed. The
mother is still being controlled and seduced into a medical context under false pretences, her power tamed.

Throughout the Western world, the best results in childbirth come from the small pockets of alternative practice
where births take place at home or in small birthing centers
that recreate conditions of home as closely as possible. This
data is readily available, and yet the vast majority of women
today are transferred from their familiar home environment
into hospital during labor. They are not ill, yet they are expected to give birth in an environment that we all associate
with sickness, injury, and pain, attended by strangers rather
than the women they share their lives with.

The very same hormones that our bodies produce during
lovemaking also trigger the physiological responses of the different phases of the birth process. In labor the neocortex or
"rational brain" becomes dormant and the "primitive brain,"
which regulates the involuntary functions of our body, is active. The hypothalamus or "primitive brain" secretes oxytocin,
the hormone that stimulates the uterus to contract, and endor-
phins, hormones that reduce pain and induce the appropriate
change of the consciousness needed for birth. They are called
the "love hormones." As in lovemaking, labor is a time for a
woman to let go of her thinking mind—to be in her body. Hormonal secretion depends on conducive human and environmental factors such as privacy, warmth, intimacy, love, and
familiar surroundings. Could a woman surrender to the passionate rhythms of lovemaking and orgasm on an obstetric

table in a room resembling an operating theater, surrounded and watched by medical personnel, however friendly or well meaning? It is equally unimaginable to give birth physiologically in such a setting, with bright lights, unfamiliar or even frightening surroundings, and strangers present. These are factors that stimulate the neocortex and actually inhibit the secretion of the love hormones.[9]

It is a testimony to the power of birth itself that occasionally a physiological birth does occur, even in such an environment. No wonder obstetrics has had to develop synthetic hormones to induce contractions. However, these widely used synthetic oxytocics are crude when compared with a woman's natural secretions, and they create unnatural conditions and risk factors that make the birth more dangerous for the child.

Under the circumstances, it is outrageous that doctors continue to inform women routinely that it is safer to have their babies in hospitals. Women are rarely informed of the risks to which they are exposing themselves and their baby in such a setting. This continues despite the huge body of critical research available to doctors. Only well-educated, middle-class women may seek out the literature now available, which gives reliable and accurate information about obstetric routines and procedures.[10]

The fact is that in an obstetrically managed birth in a hospital setting, a woman loses her power. She is passive and helpless like a beetle on its back, while her attendants control the birth. She is separated from her own body and cut off from her instinctive potential. Even at best, such a birth is a "delivery," and more often it is vaginal extraction with metal instruments or chemically controlled or surgical intervention.

Such a birth may be so traumatic for the baby that the effects can resonate through the psyche for a lifetime. Thousands of people are seeking intensive therapy to heal traumas that occurred during birth and infancy. It is well known that destructive life patterns can originate in these early experiences and seriously disturb our ability to fulfill our potential in later life.

For the mother too the normal continuum of physiological events may be so disturbed that she may have difficulty breast-feeding and parenting. Intense unresolved feelings of violation and resentment may follow a traumatic childbirth, not unlike feelings experienced by women who have been raped. These feelings can seriously disturb the relationship between mother and child unless they are well understood and resolved. The repercussions of hospital deliveries have reached epidemic proportions in our time and are wounding and crippling our society.

In every country where obstetrics is dominant, a counterrevolution exists of women's groups involved in educating the pregnant mother for birthing and campaigning for her right to give birth naturally. There are home birth support centers and a variety of relevant pressure groups and national organizations. All women, pregnant or not, midwives or not, can help to support this struggle, actively as workers or by joining their membership and supporting their activities.[11]

The medical emphasis during pregnancy must be changed to acknowledge the spiritual, emotional, sexual, and very personal aspects of having a baby. Centers can be established that provide a new social context for pregnancy, where mothers can enjoy group activities and explore ritual practices such as yoga, chanting, and drumming—practices used throughout history for the empowerment of women. These activities awaken the mother's connection to the creative forces of nature and enhance her psychic bond with her unborn child.

Birth is sacred. Time must be dedicated to healing and health, and the incredible transformative potential of pregnancy must be maximized so both mother and baby approach the birth at their best. The miracle of birth empowers all women and ensures the survival of our species. When a woman gives birth she is realizing the full potential of her sexual creativity. As she stands upright, kneels, or squats to bring new life into the world, the divine feminine is witnessed in her.[12]

The mother in active birthing is the center of power. She needs complete freedom and privacy to let herself go without inhibitions, to be surrounded only by people she loves and chooses. The power of birth, when the life force flows through the body of a woman, is awesome. She needs to surrender to the tremendously powerful contractions of her uterus, which open her body at its deepest center. The holy and radiant atmosphere that pervades a home where a child is born warms and opens the heart and uplifts the spirit. We should not be embarrassed to say that birth, like death, is a spiritual occasion in family life. When the mother has labored and given birth in a home, there is a feeling of celebration, peace, and bliss, and those who have had the privilege to be present will have a high feeling that can last for several weeks afterward.

We need to learn to accept, as women do in tribal societies, that part of the richness of the experience of birthing, like anything truly worthwhile, also involves pain. Instead of surrounding the mother with technology and drugs to eradicate the pain, we need to encourage her to accept that it is healthy and a part of the natural process of birth. Birth is like an ocean in its power. Every young girl can learn as she is growing up that there is a sea of pain at the peak of the strongest contractions in labor, which subsides into bliss and calm before the next wave rises up. When birth occurs within the family, a girl will learn this by observation, as my daughters have done. She will know that to ride these waves, a woman needs to go deep inside herself to the very core of her being. When the time comes she will be able to enter states of consciousness that are deeper, more primitive, and more primordial than the world of everyday life. When this is the case she, like billions of women before her, can find the feminine power to give birth, a power that lives inside her. She needs the freedom to move around as she pleases, to make as much noise as she likes, to breathe in her own natural way, to release and express her pain, and to experience her pleasure. She needs not to be confined or controlled.

She also needs to draw on the help of the elements during labor. The warmth of a fire burning, the help of the earth, the proximity of water—these are Nature's helpers for the woman in childbirth. She will position her body upright in harmony with the force of gravity, to allow Mother Earth to help the descent of her baby in the safest and most efficient way. This can be learned by the modern mother with the practice of gravitational yoga postures during pregnancy, so that her body learns to understand how the earth can nourish and sustain her during labor and birth.

For many women, going through the intensity of birthing without intervention has profound meaning. The mother learns about the depths of her resilience and power. In the years to come, when times are difficult with her child, she can remember these hours they went through together and it will give her strength. The power of birth lies in the wonderful, exhilarating challenge it presents to the woman, taking her beyond the usual limits of her endurance. This is a transformative experience that can be understood as a rite of passage from woman to mother. In many tribal societies it is said that a man proves himself in the hunt or in battle, but a woman proves herself in birthing.[13]

The ability to surrender to the huge and monumental waves of energy that engulf a woman's body as every fiber of her being is drawn into the involuntary reflexes of birth is a true act of shamanism.[14] Always awesome, it is not gentle or romantic, but like red hot fire, it is both agony and ecstasy.

When a woman releases the primal cries of birth—as the baby comes—they are deep and powerful, like the roar of a lioness. This universal cry unites women of all cultures in the eternal sounds of the birth-giving Goddess. Many women talk of sublime, mystical transcendental states of orgasmic release that sometimes occur as a baby is born. Could this possibly be a medical experience?

Then there is the joy, the feeling of holding a newborn baby in your arms for the very first time, one of the best things a woman can experience. There is nothing quite like this melting of the heart with love as a woman welcomes her newborn child. Later she will feel an incredible sense of pride and achievement in the fulfillment of her potential to give birth,

*UNCOILING THE SNAKE*

and she will be able to look forward to the other challenges of mothering with confidence.

There is the miracle of the newborn baby. Born without trauma, into an atmosphere filled with love and respect, the baby is alert and wide-eyed and ready for life. These are the new humans, who are born to be people of a new age. They are our future. As mothers, it is our responsibility to use all our feminine power to give birth to them safely, making sure they survive the experience physically and emotionally intact and giving them the best possible start in life.

Of course the feminine power of birth does not end with the act of birth itself. It is followed by the long period of nurturing where milk pours forth from the mother's breasts. If you ever have been to a country where breast-feeding is considered a normal part of life, you will see bare-breasted women feeding their babies everywhere. No one thinks breast-feeding is disgusting, exhausting, perverted, or incestuous. As human mothers we are mammals, and it is normal to breast-feed throughout the whole primal period (that is, from birth to three or four years old).

Breast milk is the divine food of human infancy. Isis breast-fed Horus; Krishna was breast-fed well into toddlerhood, as was Jesus Christ, if the numerous images of *Madonna di Latte* (Madonna of the Milk) that adorn Italian churches are to be taken seriously. In our modern way of life there is hardly any public evidence of breast-feeding and usually breast-feeding is inhibited or terminated prematurely.

Can we be surprised that women who have lost trust in their power to give birth might not have confidence to breast-feed? Can we be surprised that the sons and daughters who have not experienced this deep connection with the mother have forgotten the true tender source of creative power and that this leads to such disastrous disharmony, confusion, and destruction on our planet?

For too long, the feminine power of birth has been suppressed, inviting planetary extinction. The current balance of power has to change, beginning with our fundamental attitudes toward women's roles as birth givers and nurturers. We need to recognize the vital importance of women's work as mothers, which forms the heart and the keystone of our society.

Today we are seeking a return of the Feminine Force in many aspects of our way of life. This is the time when the sustaining, regenerating, and nurturing power of the feminine is of the essence, as we hope to restore and heal our world. Many people believe that the Goddess, so long asleep, is at last awakening. The changing tide is with us. It is up to us, womankind, to awaken the snake, to light the fire, to ring the changes.

## Notes

1. J. Goldsmith, *Childbirth Wisdom* (New York: East West Health Books, 1990).
2. D. Korte and R. Scaer, *A Good Birth, A Safe Birth: Choosing and Having the Childbirth Experience You Want*, rev. ed. (Boston: Harvard Common Press, 1992).
3. World Health Organization, *Having a Baby in Europe* Report on a study of Public Health in Europe — 26, (Denmark, 1985).
4. Quoted in Goldsmith, *Childbirth Wisdom*, p. 134.
5. A. Prentice and T. Lind, *Fetal Heartrate Monitoring During Labor — Too Frequent Intervention, Too Little Benefit?*, *The Lancet*, 2, no. 8572 (December 1987): 1375–77.
6. J. Balaskas, *Active Birth — The New Approach to Giving Birth Naturally* (Boston: Harvard Common Press, 1992).
7. See Goldsmith, *Childbirth Wisdom*.
8. E. Ziegel, and M. Cranley, *Obstetric Nursing*, 8th ed. (New York: Macmillan, 1984).
9. N. Newton, D. Foshee, and M. Newton, "Experimental Inhibition of Labor Through Environmental Disturbance," *Obstetrics and Gynecology* 67 (1966): 371–77; M. Odent, "The Fetus Ejection Reflex Revisited," *Birth* 14 (June 1987).
10. P. Simkin, J. Whalley, and A. Keppler, *Pregnancy, Childbirth, and the Newborn: A Complete Guide for Expectant Parents* (Deephaven, MN: Meadowbrook Press, 1984).
11. See Balaskas, *Active Birth*, for a good resource section listing main United States contacts.
12. Goldsmith, *Childbirth Wisdom*.
13. V. Noble, *Shakti Woman* (San Francisco: HarperSanFrancisco, 1991).
14. Balaskas, *Active Birth*.

# Karen Vogel

# Guardians
of the
Sacred

*Karen Vogel and I were cocreative partners in the*
Motherpeace *project in the late seventies as well as*
*coparents to my daughters; we are now living together*
*again, and she is helping to raise my seven-year-old*
*son. She continues to publish the* Motherpeace
Cards, *and we have just brought out a miniature deck*
*for the first time. Karen is an extraordinary wood-*
*carver, continuously bringing forth from the integrity*
*of the wood images that are animated and alive with*
*the spirit of the ancestors. In this piece, Karen shares*
*the intuitive way she approaches the wood, gestating*
*and bringing to birth a new sculpture.*

I carve wood because I have to. I feel like something is leaning on me and pushing me to do a particular piece. I want to bring into form a feeling or energy. This energy is embodied in the image.

Often the first response when someone sees my work is to say, "Did you find it that way?" Sometimes I have an ego twinge and think, "Do you have any idea how many hours and thirty years of woodworking go into creating something that looks like it grew that way?"

In some sense all I did was find the form within the wood. I will be drawn to carve a piece of wood to see what is inside. Sometimes I begin carving without any forethought as to what I'm going to carve; I'll just start carving and look for what it might be. I work for a while. Then I take a walk and think about the wood. Or I will sit with the piece until I get an image. As an African carver says, "They show up in my head like something coming to the surface of the water."[1]

Some of my carvings begin with pictures. When I found a postcard of "Rattlesnakes in a Dance," I wanted to carve those snakes. I assumed it was a mating dance of a female and male, and I carved the piece with this mistaken assumption. After I completed the snakes, I found out that the picture is of two males dancing. There seems to be no obvious explanation as to what precipitates this dance. The most likely explanation is that the stimulus is sexual.

Since I am a lesbian, did I unconsciously pick a perfect symbol for myself? Certainly my conscious self quite freely switches cultures, species, and gender in the images I carve. I don't know what part my unconscious played in choosing an image of what could be called "Rattlesnakes in a Homosexual Dance." I do know that I'm continually delighted by what feels like trickster energy surprising me with information about nature that is infinitely more complex and delightful than Walt Disney or biology class ever led me to believe.

Before I could begin to carve the snakes I had to study the picture for a number of months. I absorbed the form into my body and remembered times I've seen rattlesnakes. I began

*UNCOILING THE SNAKE*

to search for the piece of wood that could express the image. It meant I had to find just the right piece. It had to have a pattern and color that would look like rattlesnakes. The wood also had to be a size and shape that could contain the image.

For the past thirteen years I've carved and collected many different types of wood. So I match up images I'm carrying around in my psyche with feelings in my body and the wood in my shop. There is a final moment when those factors coalesce.

The initial focus must be quite sustained and strong, in order to overcome the density inherent in the material. The woods I often use, such as ebony, snakewood, or ironwood, are extremely hard. But the resistance is more than just a physical quality. There is an inertia in the beginning that seems to come as a challenge to me to find a way into the pattern and current running through a particular piece like water flowing down a river. The pattern turns this way and that as the tree grew, twisting, turning, and branching in response to the seasonal changes and yearly differences. Each piece of wood is unique, with a distinct temperament depending on its particular growth condition. My task is to recognize what the wood is expressing in its characteristics. The characteristics are a result of what it is (that is, hardness and color) and how it grew (that is, pattern in the rings of growth and branching). (See Fig. 7.)

My first task is to prepare the wood for carving. I cut blocks of wood off the original chunk of black walnut before I began to rough out the basic form. This is the stage where I experience difficulty in working more than an hour a day. The work looks clunky and I have to exercise a certain amount of discipline just to do it a little bit every day. I have to trust that I'll be able to transform this raw block of wood into the image I desire.

That's why I say the push to do a piece has to be sufficiently strong to get me through the first stage. The other ingredient that gives me focus is the challenge to see if I can do it. The last and perhaps strongest ingredient is love. I love wood.

*Fig. 7. Photo by Karen Vogel*

*Fig. 8. Photo by Karen Vogel*

*UNCOILING THE SNAKE*

*Fig. 9. Photo by Karen Vogel*

*This series of three photos shows the progression in Karen's sculpture of two rattlesnakes dancing, called Guardians of the Sacred. Fig. 7, the raw blocks of wood, before the artist begins. Fig. 8, the roughed-out form of the sculpture. Fig. 9, the completed sculpture of the two snakes dancing.*

*A SNAKE POWER READER*

I feel that wood is my friend, and my work comes out of my relationship with wood. Each piece is a dialogue we've had together. We listen and speak to each other and touch each other to the core. Both of us are transformed by the relationship.

During the process of roughing out a piece, I'm making essential choices in the form. I'm deciding where the snakes' bodies intersect and where their heads meet. I make these decisions based on subtle changes that I see as I uncover the pattern of the wood. As I chisel deeper into the wood I make minor adjustment in the form to reflect certain peculiarities I find. (See Fig. 8.)

As the work continues my excitement in the emerging form increases. So do the hours I work. The snakes begin to come alive. Now I enter the stage of final refinement. I'll smooth the form with tiny, inch-long, violin planes. I put in the details such as the eyes and tail rattles with my pocket knife. I'll also take out tension that I see in places in the body. The place of tension in the piece will sometimes correspond to something blocked in my body or psyche. Then I have to do work on myself or wait for a dream to release the energy that enables me to work again.

Sometimes I let a piece sit for days or weeks at a time. Wood never stops growing even after the tree is cut down. It continues to absorb and discharge moisture. The colors change too. I have also noticed how the form settles and grows into a piece over time. So when I let a piece sit and grow into itself I can then isolate the parts that are still awkward and need further refinement. Then one day the snakes are done. I've removed everything that was in the way of their coming together in their sacred dance. One of my final acts was to whittle through the last strands of wood that connected the snakes at head and neck. The cutting through came as an audible snap and a movement that left the snakes touching but not attached.

When I read descriptions of the dance I remembered that snap and movement. I realized that the head and neck form

*UNCOILING THE SNAKE*

*Fig. 10. A finished sculpture showing Karen's shamanic interest in the human-animal hybrid form, a tradition that goes all the way back to the Paleolithic and the first images of shaman-women on the walls of cave sanctuaries. Karen called this piece "The Temple of My Familiar" after Alice Walker's novel. Photo by Karen Vogel.*

the critical point of contact. The snakes push their heads together and use the resistance created by pushing to raise their bodies straight up. With this energy force they go as high as they can until they fall to the ground. The movement is repeated for half an hour or more. Through my experience of carving the form, I can clearly imagine that the dance must feel like a dynamic ecstatic union. That is certainly the feeling I wanted to bring into form. (See Fig. 9.)

**Note**
1. Richard L. Anderson, *Art in Primitive Societies* (Englewood Cliffs, NJ: Prentice-Hall, 1979).

# Naomi Newman

# Snake Talk:
# Urgent Messages
# from the Mother

*I am including two highly acclaimed theater pieces in
this volume, hoping that the reader will have enough
imagination to get the feeling of the creativity in the
work from the printed page. The first one, presented
here, is Naomi Newman's very popular* Snake Talk:
Urgent Messages from the Mother. *I deeply believe that the Goddess, as Nature, as her elemental
healing forces are pushing their way through our modern psyches, is attempting to guide us toward a more
sane way of life. I asked Naomi to lend us the Hag's
voice, since it is she who is traditionally perceived as a
direct source of Dark Goddess wisdom and who has
been demonized and negated by our modern culture.*

Snake Talk: Urgent Messages from the
Mother *is the critically acclaimed, one-woman*

*theater piece written and performed by Naomi Newman, founding member of A Traveling Jewish Theatre. It was created in collaboration with Martha Boesing, who directed it. The play opened in March 1989 at the Climate Theatre in San Francisco. It has enjoyed long and successful runs in San Francisco, Berkeley, Los Angeles, and Minneapolis. It continues to tour universities and theaters in the United States.[1]*

**A**uthor's Notes: In prepatriarchal times, the Goddess had as her ally and teacher the snake. Together they carried the wisdom of the cyclical nature of all existence. The three aspects of women—the maiden, the mother, and the crone—were seen as the Three Fates, who, in ancient peoples' mythologies, served as the creator, preserver, and destroyer of life.

As I began working on my solo piece, without conscious awareness of this material, three imperative voices emerged. One was the voice of the passionate artist, Else, who offers total devotion to the sacred act of creation. One was the voice of the Jewish immigrant mother, Rifke, from an Eastern European *shtetl*, little village, who has the obstinacy and resourcefulness necessary for preserving life under any conditions. And one was the voice of a wild, feisty street woman, the Hag, who has lived long and hard enough to speak the bare bone truths that nobody wants to hear. Midway through the process, my poet friend, Deena Metzger, pointed out that these three voices were my personal version of the Triple Goddess.

With humor and insight the three women tackle contemporary issues of aging and death, planetary survival, competition and jealousy, child abuse, and the theft of women's power and sacred teachings.

The snake's presence is experienced on several levels throughout the play: in the form itself, which is a circular winding of stories, songs, dances, reflections, and laments; in the continual transformations of the three women characters, who

*UNCOILING THE SNAKE*

over and over change from the maiden to the mother to the crone and back again; in the content, as the poet, Else, reports the messages whispered to her by the snake in her dreams. And the Hag weaves her story of a terrifying encounter with a snake around her musings on the human condition.

In the play, the Hag's appearances are surrounded by the other two characters. The story of the snake is cut up and threaded throughout the play. Each section is a commentary on what preceded it and a connective link to what follows. The end of the Hag's story are the last words spoken in the play.

*The stage is divided into three areas. Stage right is Else's writing table with journal, candle, fruit bowl, and water goblet. Center stage is Rifke's kitchen bench with chopping bowl, apron, and newspaper. Stage left is the Hag's street home improvised from old and discarded objects: wooden ladder, bundle of newspapers, garbage can cover, and large flashlight.*

## HAG: *FIRST APPEARANCE*

*(Picks up newspaper)* Oh no, shouldn't be reading this crap, you know. Bad for the digestion. Now wouldn't you think that with all of these words they could have said something useful? (*Taking scissors from pocket, sits on newspaper bundle under ladder and begins cutting words out of newspaper*) Well, we'll just do a little recycling now. Let me see if I can find something in here that's not so objectionable. (*Looking at audience*) You're out there, are ya? You know, it's not so easy to look at you. 'Cause when I'm looking at you, I know you're looking at me. And I know you don't want to see me. Come on, don't deny it. Let's not have any of that polite crap. You don't want to see me because I am ugly. Old and ugly.

(*Quieter, inward, almost trancelike*) Just like that snake in the Mojave. Nineteen fifty-eight. Scared the marrow out of my bones, all black and pussy yellow. Couldn't move, just stood there frozen scared. Boy, it was ugly. Like me, now.

*A SNAKE POWER READER*

(*Back to her matter-of-fact self, addressing audience*) You know, the other day, this fellow, he comes along and he starts up a conversation with me. And he says, "What's it like getting older?" "Older," I said, "older than what? What makes you think I know anything more about it than you do, dummy? You've been doing it since you were born."

(*Pointing with scissors to head and heart*) Think. Since I started talking to you, we have aged exactly the same amount, right? Right? Let me hear it, am I right or wrong? Right. It doesn't take a mathematical genius to figure that one out. So . . . how does it feel getting older?

Think. Most folks imagine they're getting smarter as they ripen. Then comes this mysterious moment, and all of a sudden the fruit is rotten. Folks expect you to smell bad, piss in your pants, or forget to button your bra. How come? How come? How many gray hairs do you need to slip out of the human race? How many wrinkles can you get away with before folks start talking slow, loud, and stupid at you?

You know, if most of you passed me on the street, you would either not see me or you would turn away if you did. Do you know why? Do you know why you don't want to see me? 'Cause I look like graves. I am bending down, back to the earth, getting ready for reentry. Well, you see me, and you say, "Won't be long now, she's going to drop dead. Lucky she's too dumb to feel bad about that. Lucky that's not me. Lucky I'm taking my vitamins."

(*Puts newspaper and scissors on floor and looks at audience*) I'll tell you what. I'll tell you what. You put a picture of me on your mirror, on your refrigerator door, and on your checkbook, and I guarantee you a spiritual awakening in less than a month. Study me, study me 'cause I'm studying you.

All right, let's see what we recycled this morning. (*Picks up cut-out words, shuffles them, and then reads*) "Rotten, talks, backfire, peace, erupts, the CIA, joins, the homeless." That is a great haiku, don't you think. You know, if you weren't so afraid of me, you could die laughing. You're going to die anyway, you know, you might as well get a chuckle or two.

**UNCOILING THE SNAKE**

## HAG: *SECOND APPEARANCE*

*(Sitting on chair in front of ladder)* Have you ever noticed that in order to hate yourself you gotta give yourself a lot of attention. A passing insult or an occasional barb won't do it. No, self-abuse is a full-time occupation with no time out to feed the pigeons. Metaphysical law 29J: it takes everything you've got in order to feel like nothing.

*(Inward, trancelike)* That's what happened—in the desert with that snake. It took everything out of me until I was nothing. You know, standing there I began to feel like that slimy, slithery slutch (*picks up garbage can cover and moves it up her body, as if it were the snake*) was climbing up me, wrapping itself around me, until it was whispering stuff into my ear.

## HAG: *THIRD APPEARANCE*

*(Sitting very regally on chair in front of ladder, picks up flashlight, holds it like a scepter with light directed on ceiling)* You know, there are folks who think they know what everything is about, like they think all the objects around us are made of dead stuff. But then there are the scientists, and they say it's . . . it's like, you know, carbon and helium and all that star stuff. That when it comes down here becomes oceans and cats and you and me and Mozart and Hitler and folks like that. We're all one living being. Do you get what I am saying? One living being. We humans, we are supposed to be the brains of the earth. Well, that is a little hard to believe, isn't it? I don't know. I don't know. There are lots of things I don't know, and it's a relief to say so. For example, I cannot figure out what is happening in the universe, but then neither could Einstein, so I'm in pretty good company. Most of all, though, I can't figure out what makes some folks so mean—torturing and killing animals and trees and people. But then I can't either figure out what makes some folks so beautiful, you want to fall in love with them right on the spot. I'm okay with that. I call it the Mystery. Everyone loves a mystery. Like what the hell happened between me and that snake?

## HAG: *FOURTH APPEARANCE*

*(Standing behind bench, up-center stage)* By now it was getting almost dark. I'd been standing there for hours, just eyeballing that snake, scared to death. Then something in its face started looking kinda familiar. So I said to the snake, "Do you remember me? Do you remember . . . I mean, maybe long ago we were pals?" But the snake just kept staring at me, with its tongue going *(imitates snake tongue moving rapidly)* as if it were trying to tell me something. "Oh, my God," I said. "I got it, I got it. I've got no problem with death . . . until it's my own." And then, the snake pulled in its tongue, put down its head, and we sat there a long time. Together. I think we dreamed. We dreamed that the snake was me, and I was the snake. *(Hag's body straightens and face becomes fierce with eyes bulging as she transforms into snake and remains very still for several seconds.)*

## HAG: *FIFTH APPEARANCE*

*(Moving downstage)* Now listen to the end of my story. When I woke up from that dream with the snake—you know, when we both became each other—I looked around, I wanted to tell . . . *(looks around anxiously for the snake)* The snake was gone! *(Seeing torn newspaper pieces)* But right there, in front of me, she had left me her skin. *(Picks them up, puts them in her jacket pocket)* So, I put it in my pocket, just for a little reminder. Maybe that's what it's all about anyway. Just getting rid of an old skin. *(Takes off jacket and drops it)* Let it go. *(Takes off hat and drops it on top of jacket)* Drop it. *(Revitalized, transformed, exultant)* So that something new can happen!

**Note**
1. For information regarding performances of or the purchase of Snake Talk audio or video tapes contact A Traveling Jewish Theatre, P.O. Box 421985, San Francisco, CA 94142–1985.

# *Susan Hawthorne*

# Two
# Poems

*Susan Hawthorne is an award-winning novelist and poet from Melbourne, Australia, the home of the Aboriginal peoples who call the Creator the Rainbow Serpent and say that She both created the world and is the world. I chose Susan's poems here for their evocation of the profound contact a woman can make with the invisible forces of Nature, and of the deep power of the Earth Mother in our time.*

## Dreamsnake

I sleep.
I dream of the great snake.
She manifests in many forms.
I see her coiled beneath me
    flowing under the earth
    tugging at me
    inciting me to tread the diamond track of her body.
I see her slither through the grass
    then turn and stare at me with crystal eyes.
I see her coiled about the moon
    her tail firmly grasped in her mouth
    spinning endlessly
    eternally
    through time
I see the earth open beneath my feet.
I see the rainbow light.
I am beckoned.
I watch as she approaches me
    sliding over my feet.
There seem to be two of her.
A phantom?
I feel her circling my torso
    coiling in opposite directions.
Her heads reach for my breasts.
I suckle her.
I present my own gift in return for her favor
in my ears.

© 1990

*Fig. 11. This photo was taken of a mask made at the annual Northern California Summer Solstice Camp produced by Charlotte Kelly. Photo by Catherine Busch Johnston.*

*A SNAKE POWER READER*

## *Snakes*

There are snakes living in the crevices of the rocks.
I have seen their eyes shining in the shadows.
I have heard their bodies slithering over stones.
I can see them now.
I watch.
I look into their crystal eyes.
I see a movement of a head
     a body.
I watch as one long shining body moves from her nest.
She is looking into my eyes.
Behind her I see a writhing mass of bodies.
Slowly they disentangle
    they separate
    they follow her out of the darkness and approach me
    tongues flickering.
I remain.
I am still.
I hardly breathe.
They slide forward quietly.
Their sinusoidal movements are hypnotic to watch.
There is a stillness in the air
    despite the onslaught of motion.
I feel the rasp of reptilian scales against my skin.
I do not move.
I feel their bodies pressing lightly against parts of my body
    my feet
    legs
    buttocks.
One snake runs along the base of my spine.
I shudder.
Tongues flicker and eyes gleam as they slide up over my
thighs.
Some of the snakes coil in the sun
    around the triangular perimeter of my body.

One coils in my lap.
Another spirals its way up my torso to my head.
It coils upon my crown and sleeps.
Two snakes encircle my arms like spiral bracelets.
Everything is silent again
  and still.
The snakes sleep.
I remain unflinchingly on my still spot.
I watch the shadowy movement
  of a circling hawk.
Time stands still.
The air shimmers with heat.
I am a dream.
I am a reality.
I am.
The air cools.
The spiral bracelets move.
They creep down my shoulders and neck.
The sun blazes orange and red on the horizon.
I feel a tickling in my ears.
I hear a faint whispering.
Their tongues are licking the skin
  the wax
  of my outer ears.
I hear a sound
  like fresh wind blowing
  in my ears.
I hear the distant rumble of waves on a shore.
I hear voices.
I hear individual voices breaking through the melee of sound.
I hear music
  spinning
  ringing out.
A chorus of sounds enters the silence.
I hear a voice
  an internal resonance

*A SNAKE POWER READER*

sound sliding over strings
a voice forming words
a voice speaking.
I feel the movement of my vocal chords.
I feel the words forming in my throat
my mouth.
The tongue
the palate
the teeth
the lips all in harmony.
I feel the word flutter from my mouth.
I hear myself speak.
I speak my own name.
Estelle.
I hear the sibilant hiss.
I repeat it over and over.
I speak.
I do not sing.
I do not chant.
I speak.
I call to the rocks.
I whisper to the snakes.
I feel the slither of scales on skin.
They are leaving.
I feel the final flicker of a tail as they return to their nest in
the rocks.

© 1990

*UNCOILING THE SNAKE*

*Wyoma*

# Overcoming
# the
# Fear of Snakes

*The cross-cultural archetype of woman-and-snake is older than time, linking biological femaleness to the transformative and regenerative qualities of the undulating snake who regularly sheds its skin. I'll let Wyoma's explanatory comments and Michael Michaels's photos of her holding a boa constrictor speak for themselves.*

*Fig. 12. © Michael Michaels*

**B**eing raised in the Sanctified Pentecostal Church, snakes were the symbol of evil for me and, at least to my family, were often considered to be physically danger-ous and to be feared. My family lived in the South, and when my mother was seven and a half months pregnant with me, she

*UNCOILING THE SNAKE*

*Fig. 13.* © *Michael Michaels*

was out in a field picking cotton when somebody spotted a big
black snake. Everybody scattered! While running, my mother
tripped and fell. She was told not to move, because the snake
was right there, so she lay on her back, petrified. That snake
crawled right across her belly. She figured I'd come out cursed.

*A SNAKE POWER READER*

Interestingly, as I've grown up, I've gotten in touch with an inner serpent guide and teacher named Ha, who helps me connect with my intuitive self. In the outer realm, however, I still carried that same fear of the snake as my mother had. I decided I wanted to confront that fear in the flesh. I knew the fear primarily had to do with the fact that I was raised to be afraid of snakes and that I rarely had opportunities to encounter them. So I set out to connect with a snake in a controlled, comfortable environment.

I contacted my friend Michael, a photographer who wanted to take some shots of me and who also took care of Kaa, a thirty-five-pound, red-tailed, female boa constrictor. We made an exchange. He would guide me and help me get used to Kaa, and he would photograph the process. We began slowly; I placed my hand on Michael's hand as he stroked Kaa. I was walking my coals! The energy of the snake was deeply hypnotic, intoxicating, and meditative. Within an hour's time, I'd gone from barely being able to enter the room where Kaa was draped around Michael's body, to having unrobed and let the snake crawl freely over me. I wanted to experience it fully, feeling the snake's skin against my own.

Damballa (the Voodoo snake deity) is the name of a dance performance group that I direct. I encourage the process of growth—stretching and shedding our skins by telling the truth and expressing in movement who we truly are. I have a feeling now of having truly communed with the snake and having come full circle. The photos capture the experience of going through the fear; I share them as a powerful resource of inner strength and possibilities.

# Luzclara (Machi Clarita)

# Ancient Patterns
in
Present Time

*I met Luzclara (Machi Clarita) on my first trip to Chile in 1988. We were a bit like mirror reflections for one another, both having awakened to shamanic healing energies and powers on our own, each developing her own personal teaching style for women in a particular community, both healers and ritualists working from instinct and a profound inner calling. Here Luz Clara shares the story of her initiation into the Native tradition of the Mapuche people who live at the southern tip of Chile, where they have been pushed by the onslaught of "civilization."*

I was born a rebel and like many others had to learn to swim against the current of a system that did not support my natural way of being and feeling—not my intuition and less my tenderness. So I fought everything: the system, poverty, dictatorship, imperialism, and men. I spent many years of my life believing that the only way to freedom was through fighting and struggling. During the military coup of 1973 in Chile, I was forced, along with a million other people, to leave my country with my three children and go into exile in North America. This was a very difficult nine-year period, which I spent living among the Puerto Rican and Black communities and supporting their causes, while doing much political work against the Chilean dictatorship. During this time, I was very busy, yet unhappy and angry as well. I saw that the violence I was preaching against had become part of my beliefs and way of acting, and this contradiction was reflected in the quality of my life.

I became sick and, unable to find a cure through traditional allopathic medicine, I reached out to Eastern medicine. Through acupuncture and the entire Asian concept of self, I started to take responsibility for my own healing. A whole new perspective of life appeared to me in that moment, and I began to study and learn as much as I could of this new way of thinking. Around that time, I started to meditate and feel the Spirit active in my life. I came into contact with some other women who wanted to know themselves from a deeper perspective, and we began to experiment with working in magic circles. The search was intense and changes started to happen fast.

I worked with heroin addicts in Boston and New York. This experience opened my heart in deep compassion for others and encouraged me to explore further my healing potential. I went to study herbology in British Columbia, Canada, and there I met some Native Indian people of that land. I felt at home with their ways and beliefs about the Earth, and I felt accepted and treated like a whole being. They taught me about the Earth, the Moon, the stars, the plants, the animals, the elements, the birds, and my relation to them. Something deeper was born from inside me during this time. I also met the man with whom I would later join in a mutual path of physical, emotional, and spiritual healing.

Upon returning to Boston, I knew I had to go back to Chile where my real roots and culture were. Before leaving, I heard inside me that in Chile I would be working with the feminine energy, reminding the women of their divine origins, and helping them to feel their connection with the Mother Earth and to know the Goddess within themselves.

## Back to Chile

I came home in the middle of the military dictatorship and went to live in the South of Chile, where I started an acupuncture clinic and worked with the Mapuche Indian population. I lived in retreat and solitude, entering into deep communication with Mother Earth. I learned how to grow my food, milk my cows, and make my own bread. I studied the use of healing herbs with the peasants of the area and learned how to flow with the seasons. These five years of immense purification, surrender, and healing were my preparation to start the work with the women. At the end of that cycle, I knew it was time again to go out into the world and share what the Mother had given me. Together with my new partner, we found a very sacred and powerful place in the foothills of the Andes mountains near the city of Santiago. We felt guided there and have made it into our home as well as a center where many people come for guidance and healing.

The time to start my work with women had arrived. I went into Santiago and began to offer healing rituals for women once a week. These were difficult times under the military repression, and the women were scared, sad, and dispersed. We started to work together in small groups in private homes, but before long there were over seventy women participating in these rituals within our country. To the sound of our drums, we danced, sang, laughed, and cried—emptying our hearts, which had been oppressed for so long! We felt strong together, and a deep commitment was born to each other.

This commitment culminated on International Women's Day in 1988 with a large ritual involving twenty-five thousand women in the Stadium Santa Laura in Santiago, the same place that had been used as a concentration camp and place of torture by the dictatorship. We were asked by the women political leaders to create a ritual that would join all women — peasants from the country, poor women from the slums, artists, intellectuals, mothers, young, and old — into one cohesive group of forgiveness and rebirth. First we cleaned the fear, torture, and killings from the stadium with our drums, prayers, and positive intentions. Then we celebrated our magic through music, dance, theater, and words invoking a vision of a positive future. Through our joy, strength, and hope for a future free of all repression, we healed the collective hearts of the women of Chile while expressing our power in a nonviolent way.

## The Machi

The Machi, among the Mapuche people, is the one called to be the shaman healer of bodies, minds, and souls. Only the women and a very few homosexual men are accepted into this position within their society. She is the messenger, the one who communicates with *Ngenechen*, the Mother/Father Spirit. The function of the Machi is not a personal aspiration but a divine vocation. She is chosen, usually when she is a little girl, to fulfill this mission. All Machis are called in the same way, and even if the girl doesn't know how Machis are called, she will still receive the call in the traditional way. It is encoded in her genetic memory. The Spirit of *Ngenechen*, who chooses the person to be Machi, gets in contact with the girl through her dreams and also the dreams of her parents. This call may also manifest through the *perrimonthun*, which are strange things that may happen to the girl, like finding a *kultrun* — the sacred drum of the Machi — or seeing herself in a vision going up a long stairway to the sky where she meets with the Great Spirit who announces to her that she has been called to be a Machi.

Through these experiences, she understands that her calling is to be a shaman. This is when the internal struggle begins. One part of herself wants to surrender to the calling, and the other part is afraid because she knows that being a Machi means dedicating her life to healing others. This can be very difficult, especially when it conflicts with other natural desires to be a wife and mother. It is also very expensive to become a Machi, because she has to pay an old Machi to teach her and she needs lots of silver jewelry. In the tradition of the Machis, silver pieces of jewelry are the connection with the Moon and are the sacred symbols that protect her from any negative energies while she is conducting her healing rituals. These days the Mapuche population is very poor and this can put a great strain on the family. It is a very powerful internal struggle, and a woman often tries to avoid her destiny by pretending that she is not hearing the call.

If she continues denying this call, she becomes deathly ill. Her family then calls an old Machi from the community to perform a *machitun* — a healing ritual of exorcism which has many parts and lasts for two days. It is then that the old Machi receives confirmation that the young woman's illness will disappear when she and her family accept that she is being called to be a shaman. She can only come back to life when she surrenders to serve as a Machi. It is through yielding to her destiny that she is healed.

During the next six months the different aspects of her consecration will take place. She and her family must make clothes and install the *rehue*, an altar carved from the trunk of the sacred canelo tree and having seven steps that lead up to heaven. It is through climbing these stairs, while in self-induced trance, that she connects with the Spirits and receives her healing powers. She is the messenger of the Gods and conveys the information received in trance in an ancient language, or "in tongues," which must then be translated by someone in the community who has this gift. She will also go on a spiritual

*Fig. 14. This Mapuche shaman woman is called a Machi; she stands on her ceremonial tree to play the Kultrun, which she painted with her special symbols after "blowing" her spirit into it. Illustration by Mariela Cortés of Chile.*

retreat with the old Machi and, through the oral heritage of the Mapuche people, learn the ancient magic of their healing arts and be instructed in the proper use of essential herbs.

When the young girl is ready, several ceremonies are performed that last for a few days. These are culminated when the old Machi cuts the tip of her tongue and the tongue of the young Machi and, joining them together, she transmits the old language, the speaking in tongues, which is the traditional way in which the Machi receives the messages from the Spirit. The girl has thus been consecrated a Machi. From then on her teachings will come to her through dreams.

## The Dream

From the time I was a little girl, my fantasy had been that one day I would meet an old Machi who would teach me how to be a powerful healer. When I was forty-eight years old, she appeared to me in a dream and reassured me of my destiny as a healer.* In my dream, I arrived at the house of a famous woman healer, who was wearing the traditional black dress and white blouse of the Mapuche women. She was suffering from a pain in her knee, so naturally I offered to lay my hands on her to alleviate the pain. She accepted, and when I touched her the pain went away. In that moment she said to me, "You are a healer. You have the Spirit in your hands and your energy is stronger than mine." I felt very happy and tears of joy rolled down my cheeks.

I wrote down this dream and forgot about it. A year passed and, while visiting the south of Chile where the majority of the Mapuche population lives, I met Ana, a friend who had been working with the Indian women and writing a book about traditional medicinal herbs. She invited me to go and visit Machi Antonia, who lived in a place called Dollinco, toward the coast of Chile. Two days later, the two of us and my son-in-law, Jorge, started our trip to meet the Machi. The land where the Machi lived was very dry, dusty, and almost devoid of vegetation, as is most of the land that has been given to the indigenous people of Chile.

---

*Editor's note: The astrological "Chiron return" happens at age forty-nine, marking a woman's transition to being an elder or a healer. Chiron is the planet (actually a comet) between Saturn and Uranus that astronomers call a visitor to our solar system and that in astrological lore represents the shaman or "wounded healer." Machi Clarita was called to the shamanic vocation as Chiron returned to its natal position in her birth chart. The dream came at forty-eight, and she met the Machi at age forty-nine during her Chiron return, when preparations were made for her initiation.

The first thing I noticed upon approaching the home of the Machi was her altar or *rehue* with the traditional black and white flags waving slightly in the afternoon breeze. When we arrived at the *ruka*, or thatched hut, a young Indian woman, who I later learned was the Machi's daughter, Rosa, greeted us. From behind her came an old lady in her midseventies, who was short, fat, and joyful. This was Machi Antonia. She was very happy to see Ana and told us, in a mixture of Spanish and *mapudungun*—her native tongue—that her *kultrun* had told her that visitors were coming. The Machis talk to their *kultruns* and receive messages through them in a very intuitive way. We went into the *ruka* and sat around the hearth while she started to prepare some food for us. She had only four eggs, but she gladly offered them to us.

I noticed that she was limping around, and my friend asked her what was the matter. She told us that she had injured her knee and was in pain. At that point, she noticed the drum I was carrying and asked me to play for her. She was very curious to see that I played with my hands and not with a stick, as is the custom with the *kultrun*. I played very happily and became inspired. She listened with great attention. When I stopped playing my hands were very hot, and I felt a lot of energy coming through them. Without giving it a second thought, I offered to lay my hands on her knee. She curiously accepted and sat in a chair, while I kneeled next to her on the dirt floor and put my hands on her knee. She gave a little jump like she felt an electric shock current, and looking directly into my eyes she said, "You have the Spirit in your hands. You are a Machi." In that moment, I remembered the dream and tears of joy rolled down my cheeks. I had finally met my Indian Machi for whom I had waited so long.

## Consecration

From that very moment, a deep relationship developed between the Machi's family and mine. She named me Machi Clarita and told me that since the moment she saw me she felt my gift as a healer. She insisted that there could not be a Machi without a *kultrun*, and that I had to have my shaman's drum, which she would consecrate for me. She said, "The *kultrun* is the voice that takes your prayers to the sky: she is your sister, your companion, your instrument of healing and enchantment."

During the time of preparation for this ceremony, she visited me in my home near Santiago, and I organized a big ceremony to raise money for her and her family to improve their living conditions. It was then that we decided that the full moon of April was the perfect time for the consecration of my *kultrun*. The Moon was to be the principal witness and companion in this ceremony, which was to be held at her *ruka* in front of her altar. She told me to be careful who I invited to this ceremony. She repeated many times, "If you have any doubts whether you want to invite a person or not, don't invite them. Everyone you invite will be there to give you their support, strength, and trust in your power to be a Machi."

After this, I started the process of making my *kultrun*. This was not an ordinary drum, and many special elements were necessary for its preparation. The *kultrun* of the Machi is made of the wood of the laurel tree, sacred to the Mapuche people, and the skin must be from a white female goat that has been sacrificed in a *nguillatun*—a ceremony of thanks and prayer that takes place every four years in each Mapuche community—and must be fastened with braids made from the tail of a horse also sacrificed in a *nguillatun*.

Jorge was instrumental in finding all I needed, and the day before the full moon of April, accompanied by my daughter Piedad, my dear friend Carol from Canada, and other close sisters, we started our trip in the pouring rain to the Machi's *ruka*. I was also taking with me the cloth and ribbons out of which we would make my ceremonial dress, the Mapuche silver jewelry I had been given fifteen years earlier, and an incredible two-hundred-year-old silver *tupu*—a pin—that had once belonged to another Machi and that had recently been given to me for this ceremony.

That afternoon when we arrived at Machi Antonia's place, the preparations for the ceremony had already begun. Antonia told me that her son, Santos, who is also her translator when she speaks in tongues during trance, would put my drum together the next day and that the skin had to soak overnight. She is the queen in her house, and what she says is done. From the very beginning it impressed me much how her sons obeyed and respected her. She is the Machi, the Goddess, before the mother. "In the beginning, it is not like that," she said, "but with time they understood my role of a Machi, and my husband and the children gave me their support."

That day we all worked hard. I was sewing my dress with the Machi's advice, while Rosa braided the horsehair cords—one white and one black. The Machi was making the stick to play my drum while others were cooking, chopping wood, and carrying water from the well. The ceremony started right there with us all sharing together in a common purpose—that I would have the most beautiful and complete ceremony with many blessings. The Mapuche people, like other indigenous people I have met, don't necessarily separate the spiritual from the material, and I felt that the Spirit was present in all the preparations for the ritual. We were two tribes—Indian and white—working together into the night with great joy and laughter.

We went to bed very late, but before sleeping I discussed with the Machi the name I would use in my prayers with the *kultrun* the next day. Her name had been given to her by her Machi, and I told her I had received mine some years earlier in a dream. "'Luzclara' (clear light) is not my Christian name. It is my Indian name," I told her. She said to pray like this: "'My name is Luzclara, Great Spirit, please help me. You want me to be Machi, help me.' That is the way you have to pray, in your language, the one the Great Spirit gave you, because you are not Mapuche."

At dawn, Antonia came to wake me up, and together we went to the *rehue* to salute the Sun that brings the new day and to pray for the ceremony that was to take place. She had her *kultrun* and an offering of some special drink, *muday*, which is prepared for every ceremony. I felt her strength more than ever before, and my enthusiasm grew as we played the drum and prayed for about an hour. Next came breakfast with the whole tribe, including some other Mapuche friends from the community who had been invited for the occasion.

After breakfast, she took me to a corner in the *ruka* and said, "Machi Clarita, are you sure you want to be a Machi?" "But Machi Antonia," I said, "you know I want to be a Machi. Why do you ask me at this moment?" "Well," she said, "it happens that the husband doesn't like the woman who becomes Machi; he gets very angry with her power." Then she told me the story of how her husband was very angry when she accepted being a Machi after a near-death experience. By then she was already married and had two children, and she didn't listen to the call of the Machi Goddess. "Your husband will be very angry at you when you go home," she said. I insisted I was ready to confront anything. Curiously enough, my husband was very strange and upset when I came home. I feel it is a very threatening experience for a man when the woman takes her power. But I also know that this anger comes out of fear of losing the woman. Through love and patience, I was accepted by my man in all of my power.

Meanwhile, the Machi's two sons had brought the lamb that was to be sacrificed for my ritual. This part was very difficult for me, since I don't believe in the sacrifice of blood and I don't eat meat. In the end, I yielded to their tradition and accepted this sacrifice. I stood next to the lamb and thanked him for the sacrifice of his life, and when the boys dug the knife in his neck, the blood squirted forth staining my clothes; I breathed very deeply and prayed hard. I felt that the sacrifice of this animal was to help me go back to my ancestral roots and reclaim my power as a sacred woman. The blood fell to Earth, reminding me of my menstrual blood that for many years I had offered every month to Mother Earth for the cleansing of myself and the ones around me. In that moment, I felt that much of my karma was transmuted, and the sleeping woman inside of me woke up to her sacredness.

While the preparations for the food continued and Santos was putting together my *kultrun,* Machi Antonia took me to a corner of the patio. She had prepared a special water with the leaves of the laurel tree for my purification. She poured this water over my head and body, while hitting me softly with a bunch of leaves and saying some prayers in her language. Afterward, I felt cleansed and purified.

It was then time for me to get dressed in my ceremonial clothes. Machi Antonia, my daughter, my dear sisters, and I went into the barn where, among the straw and sleeping pigs, I was dressed in my Machi clothes: a white blouse and a black wool cloth wrapped around my body and held in place with a silver pin and a cloth belt woven by the Indian women. In my hair were ribbons of many colors held in place by a headband called a *trarilonco* made of many silver coins. On my shoulders I wore a kind of black and dark pink cape held by the *tupu.* Each of the women cooperated by seeing that the ribbons were in place, the dress was evenly tied, and the silver jewelry looked very shiny. They all did their best so I would look as beautiful as possible. I felt like an Indian princess with those beautiful feminine clothes, splendid jewelry, and multicolor ribbons flying in the wind and caressing my face. Carol was saying, "If you were in North America, we would have showered you in flowers and put you in a very special place." But here I was, yielding to my destiny, sitting in the straw among the pigs.

Once I was dressed, I went to the Machi's *rehue* to pray and empty myself. I felt I could now express in words what was in the bottom of my heart. I prayed, cried, laughed, and talked to the Great Spirit. I liberated all my fears, doubts, and griefs and, while asking for strength and clarity, gave thanks for this moment in my life. Much time had passed when I suddenly realized I had been acting as if I were completely alone and had screamed and yelled at the top of my lungs. I turned around to see what other people were doing, only to find out that everyone was busy with their tasks and nobody was even looking at me. The Machi expresses herself in any way she chooses, and nobody cares how she does it. I felt so free to be myself, to be accepted the way I am. I felt very respected and supported.

My daughter Piedad approached me and said she had received a message for me. She is a very psychic person and her messages are always welcome. She said, "Mother, this is the moment in your life to leave all the doubts and fears. You cannot question yourself anymore. You are being initiated; your power as a shaman has been recognized. Take this power and use it for the good of all." I felt confirmed in what I was hearing inside myself.

By this time, the Machi's son was finishing my *kultrun*, and he invited me to go and sit by the *rehue* and fill it with all the treasures I had brought. The *kultrun* is the belly of Mother Earth, so it carries in its belly seeds, crystals, precious stones, silver, gold, copper, and many objects of power. My friends, mother, husband, and others who supported me in this initiation had given me different things to put inside my *kultrun* to increase its strength and magic. We sat in front of the *rehue*, and there in the presence of *Ngenechen* (Mother/Father Spirit), I brought out each object and, in a loud voice, expressed the symbology and the intention that it had for me in the future healing and magic I would be doing. It was then that I made the commitment to play the drum for the healing of the Earth and her people.

When we had finished this part of the ceremony, Machi Antonia and everyone else gathered around us to participate in the essential moment when I would put my spirit inside the *kultrun*. Santos had left a small opening on one side of the drum where he had not finished tying down the hide, and Antonia had told me that I was to scream my Machi invocation four times into this hole. I didn't have any idea of what I was going to yell, and my rational mind was now racing to formulate the right words. I relaxed completely, took a few very deep breaths to center myself, and took hold of the *kultrun* with a certain fixed intention. From deep within my heart, I felt a rising of inspiration, and the phrase "OM Machi OM" came into my consciousness. With the force of a true Machi, which by this time was filling every cell of my body, I screamed into the belly of the Mother four times my new mantra of power. Immediately, Santos tied off the remaining cords, sealing my spirit within it forever.

Once it was sealed, Santos gave me the *kultrun* and said, "This is your sister. Take care of her and she will take care of you." I took the *kultrun* in my hands and could feel the power and sacredness that had been given to her through this ceremony. It is now my ceremonial and healing drum, and it is with that invocation I call the Spirit every time I start to play her.

It was then time to paint the skin of the *kultrun* with the sacred symbols of the Mapuche tradition. The Machi told me that the symbols are painted with the blood of the crest of a rooster sacrificed for this purpose. I asked her if I could use red ink since I felt that symbolically cutting the crest of a rooster was against my beliefs and my work unifying the feminine and masculine energies of the planet. She laughed, because for her these energies are already united in the form of *Ngenechen,* and to sacrifice a rooster is as natural as driving a car is for someone of my culture. But in the end she consented. She prepared a red dye, and I proceeded to paint the drum. It was an experience of much power and strength, as I drew every line and every symbol with the greatest of concentration and attention to their esoteric meaning.

The *kultrun* has the form of a hemisphere, a microcosmic representation of our universe, and it is divided into four parts. The double lines that form the cross represent the four deities: Mother/Father and Boy/Girl, or as in the tradition of the I Ching, "Old Yin/Young Yin" and "Old Yang/Young Yang." These crossing lines end in the four cardinal points, North, South, East, and West. The curved lines at the extremes of the cross are the four principal phases of the Moon, and these four exact sectors determine a lunar month of twenty-eight days.

The presence of the Moon calendar in the *kultrun* comes from the lunar orientation of the Mapuche shamanic tradition. The Moon, for the Mapuche people, presides over the fertility of the Earth, the birth of her people, the determination of sex, as well as providing protection, good health, and good fortune. That is why the Machis are called *Nguenkuyen*, which means "Lady of the Moon." For that same reason, the *machitun* or healing ceremony is performed at night in the moonlight.

Between these central lines there are symbols: the Sun, the Moon, and the stars. In the center where the lines cross is the place where the Great Spirit dwells. The *kultrun* is the sum of creation, and this symbology is painted on her to remind the Machi of the Great Spirit during all her ritualistic acts.

As I infused this universal meaning into the spirit of my drum through my focused intention while painting, slowly the *kultrun* started to become alive. Once it was ready, we put it beside the *rehue* in keeping with the Mapuche custom of placing any material you receive in front of the altar to show *Ngenechen* your thankfulness. Machi Antonia gave me the stick to play it with and said, "I pass you my Spirit and my strength; may you be a good Machi."

With that the ritual ended and the feast of roast lamb, steamed potatoes, and other special dishes began. After sharing food and some good Chilean wine, which we had brought for the occasion, it was time to dance. Machi Antonia played her *kultrun* with much power and we all danced the *purrun*, the sacred dance to give thanks to the Earth. The celebration lasted a few hours with the *kultruns* and the *trutrukas*, the Indian trumpets, sending their prayers of thanks to the Great Spirit. With joy in our hearts, we connected to Mother Earth.

More than a year has passed since I was given my sacred drum, and I am slowly learning to feel her power to project my prayers and to connect me to universal strength and inspiration. The process has been concomitant with becoming aware of my responsibility as a sacred woman learning to flow with life and not to fight against or control my destiny. My destiny is of a Machi who has given her life in service to the healing of her people and Mother Earth.

I continue to work with women here in Chile and other South American countries. The awakening to the feminine consciousness has been slower in this part of the world, because we have been brought up in a very repressive Catholic society. With the recent end of the dictatorship, many new channels have been opened for women to play a part in changing our world. The old patriarchal values of our early childhood conditioning have been transformed into a new awareness of our sacredness, and like women all over the world, we are learning to live with dignity and self-respect.

## Glossary

*Mapuche.* Mapu=Earth, Che=People. People of the Earth. There are about a million Mapuche Indians in the South of Chile and the Argentinian Patagonia. They fought the Spanish conquerors for one hundred years and never surrendered.

*Machi.* She is the shaman of the Mapuche people, and apart from being the healer she is also the counselor, judge, and bridge between the Gods and her people.

*Ngenechen.* Mother/Father Spirit.

*Kultrun.* Mapuche sacred drum.

*Machitun.* Healing ritual practiced by Machis at night.

*Rehue.* Altar carved from the trunk of the canelo tree in the form of seven steps leading to heaven. Traditionally it is facing East in front of the Machi's hut. The ascending to the top of the rehue symbolizes going up to heaven to talk with the Great Spirit.

*Ruka.* Mapuche hut.

*Mapudungun.* Mapuche language.

*Nguillatun.* Community ceremony celebrated every four years by each community to give thanks and ask for peace and well-being.

*Purrun.* Dance/prayer to the Earth.

*Trutruka.* Mapuche trumpet.

## Reference

Gaston Soublette, *La Estrella de Chile* (Chile).

# Olivia Corson

# Third Stone
# from
# the Sun

*The second theatrical performance I am including in
this volume is Olivia Corson's original shamanic journey,* Third Stone from the Sun, *which I saw her
perform in San Francisco. Once a student of anthro-
pology at Yale, and now a performance art teacher in
Oakland, Olivia is a sensitive, funny performer who
uses dance and mime to tell her stories. I only wish
there were some way I could convey the use of theater
lights and Olivia's own body, as she took the audience
from this world to that one and back again. Each time
she falls into trance, she has to return from the journey and try to integrate the magical dimension into
her daily life as an urban, twentieth-century woman. I
have excerpted several bits from the piece, in hopes of
evoking the mood of the whole.*

## *Meet the Magician*

My companion and I are walking through tall grasslands at dusk. We've been traveling a long time, days, weeks. We are on the edge of a great wilderness. We lay down our packs, build a small fire, settle in for the night. We're playing cards. The only card I can see clearly is the eight of clubs. Night grows around us and is complete.

Way off on the horizon above the wilderness is a glow. I'm afraid of it. I know I must go there. I'm afraid that it's a fire of human destruction.

Huge, black winged creatures come speeding out of the forest to fetch us. They zoom toward us. They dive straight down. They level off and land. They stare at me, waiting. I get onto one of them and we take off, heading for the glow. My companion does not come along. I must make the last part of this journey alone.

I am approaching the glow. It's not a fire at all but some sort of village. From above, I see several clusters of round-houses, but I can't see any people. The bird creatures dive down. They level off and land, and they leave.

I take a few steps, looking around shyly. And then I see a man. He's fading in and out of sight. When he's still, he's so still he can disappear. He's not ready to be fully revealed to me yet, but I know he is the chief, some sort of Magician. His skin is black. He has the body of a runner, pantherlike. I can't really see his face; he's so still. But now he moves and I see that his face is composed of brilliant patterns of light and sunlit color. Turquoise and red living jewels line his face, and sunlit blues and greens stream along the gem pathways. No one can presume to just enter his village, to just start asking questions and getting answers, to find out things about this place. I know that I will not see anything more until he judges me worthy. This will take time.

Here come the black winged creatures, plummeting down from the sky, leveling off at the last second before impact. They carry me out of the wilderness, and they leave me by the dying embers of my campfire.

Weeks go by. I realize the ancient flying creatures will not come again. I must find my own way back to the Magician's village. I must find another route. I am ready to leave, to come back. . . .

HOME—where my garden is full of life and color—flowers blooming, birds singing. Home, where the California drought is still pinching in, and I feel guilty for every drop of water for my little flowers and all those long, long showers for me.

Home, where my animals will greet me with love and affection. Home, where there's animal hair everywhere—cat hair, dog hair, and fleas, fleas, fleas! Home, where my beloved may be waiting for me.

## Golden Mudfish

I'm a shepherd, a young boy. This is an ancient, hot, dry place. I'm walking over smooth, flat stones that spread out as far as I can see. Now an older man joins me, walking by my side. It is my own father, Samuel Abraham, Shmuel Abrahim. He is here with me to give me energy to move further on.

I'm flying, flying. I can see down over a vast, huge, green continent. Lower and lower I fly. There is the village. I have found my way back. I rest under one of the open, circular, thatched roof shelters. I'm weary and tired, arriving here in need.

There is just a slight motion. The Magician appears. He does not speak a word to me. I can see him a little more clearly than the first time, though his jeweled, intricately patterned face is visible and partially masked by his human face. I can't see his face clearly. I can't stare at him directly.

He has something in his hands behind his back. He presents me with two large handfuls of wet mud! In each handful is a live golden fish. Does he expect me to take this mud and to keep these golden earth fish alive? I came here for advice, for guidance. And now these fish are my responsibility?

I don't know enough. I don't know how to keep the golden earth fish alive. This task is too big for me. I'm not up to it.

The Magician has moved. He places his hand on the back of my right shoulder. His touch is softest gray. Immediately I am calm. I accept my gift, my responsibility.

The fish, the Magician, the village, the entire continent evaporates, disappears, are hidden away.

I'm ready to leave, to come back. . . .

HOME—where I can get into bed with my beloved and all my animals and listen to Jimi Hendrix. Home, where there are dirty dishes all over the kitchen, tangled clothing all over the bedroom, an avalanche of paper everywhere, junk to recycle bursting out of the back pantry, and the phone's ringing again.

## *Urban Crawdads*

. . . Next morning, eight A,M., I'm rudely awakened by the sound of people yelling and dragging things around behind my house. I'd forgotten that today is moving day for Dave who lived in a little house right behind ours. . . .

We have to drag all of Dave's stuff past our back door and along forty feet of concrete pathway running beside our house, out to the moving van parked on the street. This is the Oakland Flats. This is September. This is Indian summer and already hot. After about half an hour of schlepping Dave's stuff, I'm coming back to his house for another load and right in front of my back door, I have to leap to avoid stepping right on a creature! Its tail is arched up, its eyes are fiercely moving around on stems, it's waving its little clippers at me. It's a crawdad! My mind gropes for a logical explanation. Well, I know that ten years ago, the city of Oakland closed all its creeks. They ran all the water into culverts and smothered the old streambeds with landfill. There used to be a creek just two blocks away, and it's taken this guy ten years to dig his way up and come to me for help! I realize this is an impossible scenario. I go get an empty cottage cheese carton out, scoop him up from the hot concrete, put him into a big bowl of fresh water, and carefully arrange a brick and a stick for him. I want him to feel at home.

My friends say, "Come and look around the moving van. There's all these red, dead, smashed things. We thought they were scorpions." Red, dead, smashed crawdads are all over 46th Street! My friends go back to work, but I start to look around, and there, tucked up against the curb in front of my house, there's another live crawdad! And underneath a twisted Budweiser can, there's two more. They're all walking piteously downhill toward the bay, which is more than three miles away.

I get out my cottage cheese carton, and I scoop them up into the big bowl of fresh water with the brick and the stick. I want them to feel at home.

I look in front of our Eritrean neighbor's house. There's no crawdads. I look in front of our Hispanic neighbor's house. And in front of the Brooks's house. No crawdads. I go down as far as the crack house on either side of us. No crawdads. All of the live crawdads are in front of my house, and now there's fourteen crawdads in three big bowls of fresh water with their bricks and their sticks. I want them to feel at home. However, I do not feel at home. I feel like I'm losing my mind. I say, "Goddesses, I want to save the planet. I want to save the animals. But don't send them to my front door. I can't handle it."

At the end of the day, we load up the three big bowls of water with the fourteen crawdads and the bricks and the sticks and we take them up to Redwood Park. We search until we find a muddy pool of water in the drought-parched streambed, and we release them with a sort of good-bye sunset ceremony, and all the crawdads scramble down, falling over each other in their haste to get into the dark water. "Good-bye! Good luck! Don't come back!"

Now it's pitch dark and we're driving home. This strange day is over, right? Wrong. . . . In front of my house, in front of my car, lit up in my headlights, there's two more, waving their clippers. "You missed us! We're dying of thirst, and all day long, all the others died and got smashed, and we hid here in front of your house waiting for you to find us and rescue us!" With unsteady hands, I get out my cottage cheese carton and I scoop them up into the big bowl of water with a brick and a stick. I guess I want them to feel at home.

We kept these guys for almost a month because I didn't have time to go back to Redwood Park and release them. Every day, I'd check on them. I'd slide the board off their bowl of water. The reaction was always the same—mutual alarm. I'd jump back. They'd dive for the side of the brick. They're so strange. All those extra legs, and their tiny eyes attached to stems; little armored aliens! I fed them cat food and they were strange houseguests.

I'm falling, falling.

## *The Sourceress*

Again, I am the shepherd. I am walking along a river, a very familiar place. I'm playing in the water. There is my grandfather, waiting for me. We laugh together and we dance together in the perfect sunlight that plays through the green leaves.

A large hawk dives down, grabs my right shoulder, and lifts me up. My *zeda* (grandfather) is waving good-bye. The hawk is flying over the world. There is the vast green continent far below us. The hawk dives down over a large body of water and he drops me, and somehow I catch an air current and I'm floating. There she is; the Sourceress, the Magician's wife.

She's canoeing. She's very strong. Her black skin is glistening. She's alone, at peace in her work. She's singing. She knows that I am here to watch her and learn from her. She tosses up red and yellow sands to me, which carry the smell of honeysuckle in the rain, of red raspberries. She is keeping me in alignment with her so that I can follow her and not interrupt her ongoing work, her rhythms.

She takes a small golden bucket, and she lowers it down into the water. She's calling, calling. When she brings the bucket back up, it's all full of little octopuses. They're all dancing around excitedly. The Sourceress is laughing, but now she's checking them closely, counting them, noting their health, their sizes, their colors, their genders. She's listening to them, watching the way that they move, gently touching them, smelling them, tasting the water. Now she knows just what balancing elements are needed here. She lowers the bucket back down into the ocean, and the octopuses swim away. Then she measures out an exact handful of deep blue stones and she sows these weighted droplets into the water. She is the chemist. She is the chemist and the alchemist of this realm, working to maintain the chemical balance necessary for all oxygen-based Earth life to continue.

She's moving on, but here comes a large alligator swimming rapidly toward her boat. It swirls and spins around her. It is very aggressive. She tries to adjust herself. She tries to stare at it and face it. It's much too big to defend against. It could easily chop her boat right in half, but as she adjusts herself and continues to face it, it begins to change into two parts—an alligator and an old woman somehow bound up together. The Sourceress is laughing. She knows this creature. She knows the old woman. It is her own mother coming to visit her. She helps the creature into her boat, wraps it in a plain, thick, gray blanket. She paddles to shore, lands the boat, unloads the creature, and opens the blanket. The two parts have separated. The alligator part moves swiftly and strongly back into the water, leaving behind a very old woman with pale skin and piercing blue eyes.

The Sourceress wraps her mother back up in the blanket and builds a small fire, and the two women begin to sing a sunset song, a warming song. From underneath the blanket, the old woman pulls out a bowl of deep red stones, and then she pulls out a rattle, a gourd rattle. Out of nowhere, she produces a large mask, an alligator mask, magnificent in detail with teeth and eyes. The old woman hands the mask to her daughter, who puts it on. Night is complete. The old woman keeps time and her daughter begins to dance. The old woman takes the deep red stones and hands them to her daughter who hurls them out into the night again and again.

Two women are building . . . a red cave. It's a nest for a baby. Together the two women are making the entire night forest fertile for the next season's growth. Together the mother and daughter are cycling old age and death back into birth for all the life forms on Earth through this night dance.

I'm ready to leave, to come back.

HOME—where I'm going to get organized this year and put everything where it belongs. Home, where I can't think of where everything belongs. I don't have the slightest idea of where everything belongs. Everything is just wherever it wants to be. Home, where I can daydream and remember.

## Story Creatures

I like to cook in the middle of the night when I can't sleep. I like to cook and sing. And I like to think that the smells from what I'm cooking waft themselves to my front door, drift and dance up and down my street, and any of my neighbors here in the Oakland Flats, who may also be having just a touch of insomnia, they smell these glorious smells from what I'm cooking. They grab their beautiful, homemade, ceramic, carved bowls; they come to my house, and we sing together and break bread as the dawn comes up.

Anyhow, I like to cook for no one in the middle of the night, and I think. And lately I've been thinking about the human niche. I'm so fascinated by all the other animals; I always have been. What are we? What are we here for? Is it just to build bigger and better and faster machines? To relentlessly seek out and exploit new ways of selling useless crap to disheartened humans? I refuse to accept that. What makes us unique like all the other animals?

We've got these hands, these thumbs, these imaginations: manifestations of our need to make things, to create. We are so naked and vulnerable. So relatively slow and helpless. We've gotten really preoccupied with making things to cover up this vulnerability—fast cars, big weapons, lots of lights, lots of stuff, lots of money. . . . But lately in the dark of the night, here in the Oakland Flats when I can't sleep and my heart races, I just know that if we survive, we will learn to make the most beautiful things—a rainbow technology that goes soaring over the canopy, not harming the wilderness and the complex life below, so that once in a while when we slow, naked, easily bored, usually scared humans need to, we can get up above it all and look around and make up songs and dances.

Singing and dancing. Now, lots of creatures sing. Birds sing. Dolphins sing. Wolves sing. Certain whales can send the deep-toned vibrations from their complex songs one thousand miles through the ocean to their fellow whales. But when humans sing, they change themselves.

My dog dances when she's hungry or excited. Bees dance. Lots of birds dance. Dolphins dance. Certain spiders dance very precisely on the edge of their webs so that their potential mate recognizes them and doesn't eat them. But humans, when humans dance, we change ourselves.

And we have these unique memories with thousands of years of coded information and stories, symbols, and evolution dropped into our every cell, and the files and decoders stuffed into our little infant brains. And we spend our whole lifetimes sorting through all this stuff trying to find and form the one story that is ours alone, that we can and must tell.

Perhaps we are the only creatures that learn through stories, that live through stories, that understand and heal through stories. I love that story about the young King Arthur and his teacher, Merlin. And in the final teachings, Merlin changes Arthur into various animals so that he might learn, so that he might become a great king. And in the final transformation, Merlin changes Arthur into a northern bird, and Arthur flies far, far away from his human self. He is a free bird, mated for life, and he gets so far away from his human self that Merlin has to call to him kind of gruffly to get his attention.

"Arthur! Arthur! Pay attention to me! Now look down and tell me what you see."

"I see the rivers and the creeks. I see the forests and the valleys and mountains. I see the deserts and the ice, the clouds and the oceans. There are no human boundaries. There are no human countries. There is one Earth. There is one Earth."

I'm falling, falling.

## Third Stone from the Sun

I dance. I move. I am seen and heard. Beautiful complex music from the soul and passion of my husband surrounds me. From out of an old flower-printed pillowcase comes my new, ancient, powerful, gentle snake friend, Cherokee, daughter of Isadora. The weight of her perfect body undulates across my back, the cool satin pattern of her skin glides across my throat. Her small, quick tongue takes information from my cheekbones, my eyelids, my forehead. Her head rises one foot, then two feet above mine, seeking the moist, hot canopy of her ancient forests, of her free ancestors. Together we dance, clearing space, blessing one another, re-membering. Inside the slow, moving majesty of her long body—intertwined with this ancient living relative of my young, warm-blooded species—I breathe and I am, we breathe and we are, once again, pure Earth magic. L'chaim—to life! I'm ready to leave, to come back. . . . Home.

*N. Susan McClees*

# The Initiation

*N. Susan McClees works as a shamanic counselor and healer in San Francisco. Her poem, "The Initiation," is a mythical representation of the arduous path that has brought her liberation.*

A desert camp
A bed in the rocks
A timeless place of stone canyons,
 streaked with color, cracked with storm.
Monoliths jutting up,
 ageless witness to millennia of existence.
Nothing civilized here.
This is where the earth stores its wisdom.

It is night.
The lizards and birds have ceased their playing
 and have fallen silent.
Everything has a sense of portent,
A dark stillness of anticipation.
A fecund moon slides between tatters of clouds.
There
 on the desert floor
Something stirs.

A woman
Naked
Her skin bathed in silver light
Moves among the rocks.
Her body muscular, smooth
 her breasts pendulous, swaying.
Her purpose known to her for eons
But denied by the outer world
 for almost as long.
Her appearance is at once mystical, unknown,
 and familiar.
She turns and looks at me.
What weighty knowledge
 is emanating from within her?
What arcane secrets
 pulse in her veins?

*UNCOILING THE SNAKE*

Who is this Artemis
    who stirs ancient memories in me?
Who causes me to feel
    long-denied power?
I am frightened by my own awakening
I am drawn to her with no choice,
    tears burn my cheeks.

Her face turns toward me,
    my throat is tight
From her flashing eyes
    a strong swift certain light
Silently penetrates my core.
Will I survive this?
The heavy crust of deception
    is breaking off my spirit.
Its jagged pieces cut me as they fall.
The false myths
    of weakness,
    worthlessness,
    dependence
Clutch
    as they are torn away.
The lies scream
    as they are seared off.
The centuries of deception
    bred into my flesh
Lie ruptured and bleeding
    on the desert floor;
Their essence leaking away
into the sand.

My soul is scoured clean.
I am transformed into the silent knowing.
I am forever changed.

*A SNAKE POWER READER*

# Bonnie Benson

# The
# Manu

*When* Snake Power *was functioning as a quarterly magazine, we accepted manuscripts, some of which lay dormant until I contracted with Harper to do this book. One day I got out the files of old submissions and looked through them for the first time in three years, and this story by Bonnie Benson, a writer and translator living in Costa Rica, touched my heart. I am pleased to include it here as an expression of the ancient patterns that insist on pushing through us, regardless of our culture, status, or gender protocol. Women today are finding ourselves compelled to express through channels that have been forbidden to us for centuries, in order to be a part of the necessary healing of the earth.*

Ilearned to sing the song when I was very young and the Manu was very old. He was teaching it to Graf who was to take his place. Graf was my brother and I followed him everywhere.

"The song is sacred, not to be sung by woman."

"She won't sing it, she knows the law of the tribe."

"If the song is ever sung by woman, great evil will fall upon us. The power of the song will be weakened."

So Graf promised that I would never sing the song and I was allowed to follow. As the Manu sang the songs, I learned them much quicker than Graf. To him, they just seemed to be words that he had to learn, but to me they were alive. I knew the people, they were real to me. Often, when the hunters were gone, I would go off by myself and sing the songs. At such times, the power of them would come to me and I would see and feel the people and their feasts. And their courage and passion would fill me and possess me. At such times, I could see the future. I knew when the hunters would return and what they would bring.

Then bad times came. The weather became colder and ice was everywhere. No matter where we went, there was ice and snow. The hunters spent all their time searching for food. There was never enough, and the women and children became thin and sickly. The hunters came to the Manu and asked him to sing the song, to ask the spirits for help. At first, the Manu resisted.

"To sing the song requires great strength, great power to contain the spirits. To sing the song is a dangerous matter."

"But the people are starving, Manu. We must do something. Let me sing the song," Graf said. Finally the Manu called a council. All the hunters came.

"It is time to sing the song. I am old and may not survive the singing of the song. Graf will sing and I will be with him."

The hunters had made a great fire, and Graf and the Manu stood in front of it. In the night, the fire was bright and threw strange shadows everywhere. The women stayed in the tents with the children, many of whom were dying. I was there behind the hunters, but no one paid any attention to me. Everyone was watching Graf and the Manu.

Slowly the Manu began the ritual. I watched closely because although I knew the songs, it was the first time I saw the movements that accompanied the words. Graf stood next to the Manu and was guided by him. They circled the fire three times, singing the calling song in a low voice. I could hear Graf stumbling over some of the words; they were still not alive to him. Then the Manu moved to the opposite side of the fire from Graf and lifted his arms. Both seemed to be trying to remember the words, words that flowed through me and begged to be sung. I moved closer to the circle, and the hunters who were in a trance didn't notice me. Together Graf and the Manu started to sing the spirit song. The Manu's voice was weak with age, Graf's timid with fear. Inside me, the words were welling up and I could feel the power of the spirits around me. I knew they couldn't enter me unless I said the words aloud. I covered my mouth and watched the spirits enter Graf. His eyes opened but he couldn't see. Terror shot out of them. A man does not know how it feels to be entered, a man's spirit cannot make room, cannot expand to include more. Graf's body went rigid and then fell.

The Manu watched, his arms still raised. I could feel the spirits swirling, looking for a body strong enough for them to enter. The Manu was too old, too weak. It would kill him just as it had Graf. Then I heard the Manu's silent cry. He asked the spirits to find a strong body. The spirits surrounded me, tearing my hand from my mouth, entering me. And I sang the spirit song.

The words came from me with power and the hunters around me stepped away. My voice carried even to the women in the tents. With every word, the power grew and the visions became clearer. The fire into which I stared was a spark

*A SNAKE POWER READER*

compared to the passion that seized me. The past and its heroes came alive and carried me into the future. And I spoke the visions to the hunters.

Many years have passed since my first singing of the song. Our hunters bring us much meat and the children are fat and healthy. Because I am a woman, they will not call me the Manu or give me the robes except to use for singing the song. The hunters have begged me to teach the song to a young man. But my answer is always the same.

"Only the Manu can teach the song."

*UNCOILING THE SNAKE*

# Rachel Pollack

# The Body
# of the
# Goddess

*Rachel Pollack and I met years ago as a result of our mutual interest in the Tarot and feminism. When she sent me the first few chapters of her forthcoming book,* The Body of the Goddess in Landscape, Temple, and Art *(London: HarperCollins) I was struck by a synchronicity of our current exploration and felt that an excerpt from it would be perfect in this collection.*

*I have recently begun to travel internationally and to prepare women's group pilgrimages to sacred sites around the world. Some time ago I began to feel an impulse to see the temples on the island of Malta, and I had a significant dream.*

*I'm in Malta with my family. It seems quite strange to me, quite odd and unusual. I feel like I want to start going around to the sacred sites, there are so many here. I see a framed picture hanging in a room in this house that seems to suggest we are near two special ruins that resemble Stonehenge and the men-a-tol.*

*I look out the window. It's twilight. There are mountains around the outside of the island that look so muted and mysterious, like flat hills cut off at the tops, like old volcanoes, just old and weird and totally powerful. I'm awestruck, speechless, silenced by the beauty. I stare, quieted and peaceful, and I sigh, and mention the incredible beauty.*

*I am drawn out onto the land. We get into a car and drive. Off to the left there is an amazing, unbelievable creature flying — it looks like a combination of the vultures off the walls in Catal Hüyük and the Chinese character for "change." I burst out, "Wow!*

> **I Ching sign for "change" and vulture priestess from wall of Catal Hüyük.**
>

*Look at that! It's one of the vulture priestesses flying right here before our eyes!" I'm so struck by the strangeness of this place, and this exotic creature just flying along on the side of the road. My family seems unable to really notice, to really receive into themselves what they are seeing. They remain dense and negative. I feel childlike and open.*

I am drawn to the Mediterranean for reasons that exist below the zone of my rational consciousness, and traveling there awakens an old memory in me about the ancient world and the worship of the Earth as Goddess. The Malta dream also seems to *function as an oracle, reminding me of my childhood feelings of alienation from those around me who were less attuned to the ancient, sacred ways.*

*When I visited Malta, I discovered that the description in my dream related to the second, smaller island of Gozo (with its flat, conical hills) where the more ancient temple, Ggantija, was built in the fourth millennium B.C.E., making it the oldest known stone temple in the world. Ggantija means "female giant." The temple is in two parts, each shaped like the female body, one larger and one smaller. This constellation has led Marija Gimbutas to posit that the temples represent perhaps the divine mother and daughter, or sisters, as was found in Catal Hüyük in ancient Turkey.*

*Rachel's work articulates so carefully and lovingly this phenomenon—that we are part of a living Goddess, whose visible body is our planet and ourselves.*

What does it mean to write about the body of the Goddess? To concern ourselves with the body, to think the idea, to try to conceive (a word coming out of women's bodies) of God(dess) having a body? For many people the idea is alien, almost unthinkable.

A sacred calendar published some time ago listed, among Pagan seasonal rituals and the holidays of the established religions, the birthdays of various deities from ancient Greece and other cultures. April 28th was given as the birthday of the Buddha and the Goddess Artemis (whose body fills these pages even as Her body rises still in the hills and mountains of Greece). To celebrate Artemis I went to a waterfall in the mountains near my home. When I told people what I had done, many of them looked surprised or even laughed. "Artemis has a birthday?" they asked. Now, some of these people were Pagans who actually worshiped Artemis as the Roman Goddess Diana. And others would have had no trouble with the Buddha having a birthday since, after all, he was a mortal man, Prince Siddhartha. And most of these people have celebrated the birthday of Yehoshua ben Yosef, a radical Judaean who claimed to be God's son and whose followers claimed he was the messiah, or christ. And yet the idea of a Goddess, a wholly divine being, actually being born struck them as bizarre.

The newly (re)awakening religion of the Goddess is a religion, and a movement, of basic realities, of birth and death, of the cycles of the Moon and Sun, of menstruation and pregnancy. Gertrude Rachel Levy, author of *The Gate of Horn*, characterized religion as the maintenance of "an abiding relationship."[1] This relationship breaks down and religion becomes superstition, or perhaps philosophy, when we lose that original relationship to the divine in the physical world—when ideas and symbols become detached from bodies.

The body is our fundamental truth, and the body of the Goddess is fundamental to our relationship to the divine. The African Goddess Oya expresses Herself as lightning and as rivers. The prehistoric Goddesses of Europe and the Middle East took the forms of fish or bees or trees or toads or vultures. To us today these images seem strange, even childish. We are used to thinking of God as an abstraction. As archaeologist Marija Gimbutas and others have shown, all these images came from a deep and specific understanding of animals and plants and the processes of life married to a spiritual awareness that worked in people's lives at all moments.

The abiding relationship extended to all aspects of life. When James Mellaart and others excavated a ten-thousand-year-old city near the village of Catal Hüyük, Turkey, they found Goddess statues like pregnant women set atop bread-baking ovens. This too strikes us as bizarre, but think: isn't bread and all cooked food a miracle? Various ingredients are mixed together and shaped into a particular form (how wonderful it would be to know the forms Neolithic people chose for bread!); the mix goes into a hot closed container; and something totally different emerges, something life-giving and sensually satisfying. And think of the miracle of pregnancy, of a fetus forming and growing like bread in the hot darkness of a woman's body. We have lost the sense of the miraculous in the everyday things of life precisely because we have tended to see God as abstract, remote, somewhere out there—detached from bodies.

And yet, a common expression shows the survival of an ancient idea. We describe a pregnant woman as having "another bun in the oven." Does this phrase go all the way back to prehistoric Turkey? The idea may seem farfetched, but Gimbutas has shown the value of comparing archaeological remains to country folklore.

Even love has become abstract. We think of "true" love as a pure essence and physical love as suspect, a trick or illusion, even dirty. "God is love," we say, but since God does not have a body, divine love must not be contaminated with physical desire and satisfaction. In other cultures and times, this separation is unknown. Aphrodite, Goddess of sexual love, was also a Goddess of birth and death, of the surging sea and the birds of the sky. She was a mother of change and becoming as well as passion, and she was connected to those ancient female-centered cultures of Anatolia, Turkey. Over the centuries the patriarchal Greeks narrowed her power, limiting her image to a petty courtesan. Paul Friedrich, a writer on myth, tells us that Aphrodite inspired passion in heterosexuals and lesbians, while her son Eros enflamed homosexual men.[2] It tells us something about our culture's attitude to women that the term for sexuality is *erotic* and not *aphroditic* and that the names Aphrodite and Venus—Venus is the Roman name for Aphrodite—survive in such negative or trivial sexual terms as *aphrodisiac* and *venereal* disease.

When the Christian religion took over, Aphrodite was banished. According to Friedrich, most of the Greek deities became saints in the new religion, except for Aphrodite, who simply disappeared. Even diminished, the reality of her (female) body threatened the Christian paradox—that of an all-male deity who at the same time had no body.

Christian myth describes angels as disembodied and sexless. And yet they are also male, with masculine names still in use today, such as Gabriel and Michael. Maleness became separated from sexuality, with "reason" the primary male quality. Abstract and bodiless, masculine reason must control the body, which stands always in danger of contamination, especially from women. When God becomes detached from physicality the goal of humans becomes to escape the "prison" of the body.

It becomes almost impossible to think of God's body, certainly as anything more than a metaphor. In many cultures, such as the Jains of India, there is a tradition of seeing the universe as a single body. In the Jewish esoteric tradition of Kabbalah we find not only the image of Adam Kadmon, the cosmos as a great primordial being, but even an idea called "Shiur Komah," or Measurement of the Body, in which mystics tried to discover God's physical measurements. Gershom Scholem, the great scholar of Kabbalah, described this idea as "absurd" and "monstrous," though he also described it as inspired by the Song of Songs and its description of the Body of the Beloved.[3]

Presumably, Scholem knew that the idea was not unique to the Jews. As well as the Jains, with their very precise measurements of God's lips, toes, elbows, and so on, many cultures tell the story of the physical world having been formed out of a single body, the body of a Goddess. In many versions of this myth, She is dismembered, broken apart into millions of pieces, often by male violence. These are myths from male-dominated cultures, and they raise many complex issues. Beyond the tearing apart, or the Goddess falling to pieces, we find a deep intuition—that the cosmos and everything in it, every rock and drop of water, is alive, like we are, and is female, like the mothers who gave us life.

Over a period of years, and through the influence of friends and books and my work with the Tarot, I had become interested in the religion of the Goddess and wanted to deal with this subject in my work. I knew as well that many people were reviving the practice of sacred journeys by traveling to power places and ancient temples in many countries. Some ten years earlier I had visited several caves in France that contain engravings and paintings created as much as twenty thousand years ago. That experience had moved me deeply, and I knew I wanted to go back and see these works in a context of sacred knowledge.

Almost immediately I came across an amazing concept. In various places, particularly on the island of Malta, the temples dedicated to the Goddess were themselves shaped like a simplified drawing of a woman's body—with rounded chambers, like breasts and hips, and a smaller chamber at the back for a head. The worshiper who entered them felt herself enter an actual divine body. Women who had traveled to Malta described feeling overwhelmed by a sense of protection, of love.

But it was not just human constructions that were seen to carry the shape of the Goddess's body. The land itself could take such a form when viewed in the right way. In an article by architect Mimi Lobell (the same article where I read about Malta) I came across an idea first put forward by Vincent Scully, professor of architecture at Yale. Scully found that the so-called palaces of ancient Crete (the term *palaces* betrays assumptions of monarchy that have never been proven) were set in particular landscape formations. Each of the large buildings was sited (roughly) on a north-south axis facing a conical hill and beyond that a horned mountain containing a cave used as a religious sanctuary. In Lobell's words, "The proper siting of the palace accentuated the meaning of the landscape as the body of the Goddess. The valley was her encircling arms; the conical hill, her breast or nurturing function; the horned mountain, her "lap" or cleft vulva, the Earth's active power, and the cave sanctuary, her birth-giving womb."[4]

This idea captivated me. Like many people, I had earlier suspected that the concept of the Great Goddess was a modern invention, a feminist myth. Though my early reading changed my mind and showed me the solid research behind the image of the Goddess, it was the ideas of Lobell and Scully that gave the Goddess a concrete reality. This was a reality I had never experienced in the traditional religious ideas of my own society.

I began to read and to think about the Goddess, about Her body, her presence in the world, the connection to my own body and to women's bodies in general. The use of caves as sanctuaries suggested a link to the prehistoric art caves of France and Spain. If the Earth is our Mother, then a cave becomes an image of her womb, a place to enter Her actual body. Was this why the Cro-Magnon artists chose to paint and engrave their work in caves? There is no way to know. They left no record other than the art itself. When I read Joseph Campbell on the caves, I found the idea that the entrance to Lascaux cave, the greatest of the art centers, was a long tunnel, so narrow an adult had to crawl at places, and it was marked with female symbols. Thus, according to Campbell, the tunnel becomes a birth canal in reverse, and the great hall a womb alive with animals. I have not seen this idea elsewhere; the original entrance to Lascaux caved in thousands of years ago, so it is not clear whether the entrance found by a group of boys in 1940 actually was used by the painters. (Visitors today enter a large unpainted chamber where they wash the soles of their shoes and then pass through a human-made door directly into the great Hall of the Bulls.) Nevertheless, the idea stuck with me, so that when I read more about the caves I compared them to the inside of my own body. And when a friend and I visited the cave of Pech-Merle, with its huge tunnels and chambers and its walls dripping red, both of us (independently) felt like microbes inside a gigantic body.

In many mountainous areas certain peaks will resemble a face in profile or a woman lying on her back, and folklore will often make this link explicit. However, there are other ways to

*UNCOILING THE SNAKE*

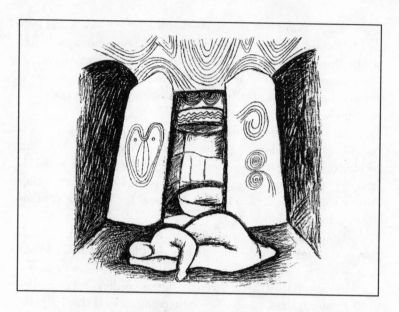

*Fig. 15. This is a drawing by Scandinavian artist Monica Sjöö, illustrating the so-called "Sleeping Lady" of Malta. The underground chambers at Malta were used for dream incubation and, more precisely, to call in the ancestral spirits to the body of a pregnant woman who would sleep there overnight. Monica Sjöö is author of* The Great Cosmic Mother *(HarperSanFrancisco, 1991), which contains many more of her paintings and illustrations.*
*The Sleeping Lady of Malta, by Monica Sjöö.*

see the Goddess as physically present in the land. The indigenous people of North America have always seen the Earth as the mother of all her people — with *people* including the plants and animals as well as humans. When I was growing up I learned that Native American men refused to become farmers because farming was "women's work." In fact, as I learned much later, the Native people resisted farming because it involved cutting their mother's breasts with a knife.

As well as the idea of the land as the Goddess's body, I knew of traditions that saw other aspects of nature as essentially female because of their symbolic resemblance to women's physicality. Many cultures have identified the Moon as a Goddess, directly linked to women's bodies. (Some books will describe this connection as a universal idea. However, universal ideas rarely exist; the ancient Japanese and Germans were among the minority of cultures that saw the Moon as male and the Sun as female.)

Most obviously, most women's menstrual cycles are roughly the same length as the Moon's cycle from new to full to old to new. Recent studies in college dormitories and isolated villages have suggested that a group of women living closely together will tend to menstruate at the same time, often during the full Moon.

There is a more subtle connection as well. The Moon moves through three distinct phases. It is born out of darkness as a sliver that steadily increases until the magnificence of the full Moon, and then, after three days, it dwindles and dwindles until finally it dies, vanishes for three days, and then is born once again. Women (and, of course, men) arrive in the world out of the darkness of their mother's womb. They grow as maidens until, unlike men, they come to a sharp division in their lives — menarche, the first menstruation. They remain fertile, capable of the miracle of growing children in the darkness of their own bodies, until another distinct break (though a gradual one), menopause.

These phases — maiden, mother, crone — seem a natural comparison with the waxing, full, and waning Moons. The various Triple Goddesses in different mythologies (especially European) have given the identification a powerful presence in the modern religion of the Goddess. Wiccans, or witches, worship the Moon, not as a celestial body but as a manifestation of female truth and power.

When we think of the Triple Goddess we tend to think of ancient Greece or Celtic Ireland. However, Marija Gimbutas has pointed out that the image goes back at least to the Magdalenian period in France, some twelve thousand years ago, for the cave of Abri Du Roc Aux Sorciers, at Angles-sur-Anglin,

*UNCOILING THE SNAKE*

France, contains a relief of what Gimbutas terms "three classical female presences with exposed vulvas."[5] From 3200 B.C.E. we find a more abstracted triple image, a magnificently carved triple spiral on the curbstone at the entrance to the huge passage "tomb" of Newgrange, in the Boyne River valley of Ireland.

And there are other links between nature as a whole and women's bodies. The Earth gives forth plants in the way women give forth babies, out of a hidden darkness. Here too we find a promise of rebirth, for the same plants that seem to die in Winter return in the Spring. A baby growing in its mother's womb floats in a sac of liquid, and when the woman gives birth the water breaks. So now we find two red flows, menstrual and birth. We begin to see the source—physical, not just intellectual—of the link between women and water, the seas, rivers, even springs.

The sea surges and falls like the inner rhythms of a woman's body. Just as the Moon appears to govern menstruation, so it causes the rhythm of the tides. The seas are salty, like the tears and blood of women's (and men's) bodies. And as far as we know today, all life originally came from the seas.

At the beginning of the work I sought the Goddess's body in the most literal way, looking for mountains that appeared like breasts or the profile of a woman lying on her back. Very soon a more subtle idea began to present itself. Landscape formations of the Goddess might have other characteristics, such as different mountain shapes or alignment with north and south. Temples and stone circles might be in the form of a woman's body, but they also might function as landscape markers or as calendars to record the solstices, equinoxes, or other moments of the year.

First I assumed that the Goddess's "body" meant her shape in the land and temples. I have come to see the body as whatever comes into existence in the world. Sitting in the hills of Delphi in Greece or walking among the limestone crevices near the Teaching Rock of Peterborough, Canada, or entering the darkness of passage mounds in Northern Europe or taking part in a ritual in a city apartment to celebrate the coming of Spring, one becomes aware that the body is more than an object. The body encompasses all our experiences. The body of the Goddess is not just the forms of the Earth or the stars, but their qualities and their meaning.

The Goddess has both a visible and an invisible body. Both of these are mediated by culture. That is, humans have designated certain animals or certain landscape forms or certain artistic images as especially evocative of the Goddess's physical reality. Her visible body is in the landscape; and in temples, in trees, especially sacred groves and particular species of trees. Her body takes shape as well in animals, but especially those seen as expressing Her special qualities. These include pigs, sheep, bears, birds of prey, and especially cows, bulls, and snakes. The visible body is also the sea, source of all life, whose salt water matches our blood. We find Her body in rivers and streams and in the rain, without which we cannot live.

The visible body expresses itself, emerging into being, in sexuality—the procreation of animals and plants, the electric sex of sky and earth in thunder and lightning, and the vast variety of human sexual experience. And here the Goddess religion, both ancient and modern, differs sharply from the religion of the transcendent God. For if God has no body and exists apart from the universe that He has created, then human beings become souls that either possess bodies, like objects or clothes, or else become trapped in bodies, prisoners in a cage of flesh. And religion becomes a yearning to escape the body as well as a command to control it.

Influenced partly by modern ideas of sexual freedom (which in turn derive partly from encounters with tribal peoples) and partly by the sexual images from the ancient Goddess religions, the contemporary religion of the Goddess has opened sexuality as a sacred expression. "All acts of love and pleasure are my rituals," wrote Starhawk—a manifesto of liberation in a single sentence.[6]

We find the Goddess's body in birth and in menstruation, especially when we give these physical functions a sacred and ceremonial value. We find Her as well in disease and death, for these are not mistakes or punishments but are part of existence. If we compare the mythologies of Goddess-centered Crete and the later, patriarchal religion of the Greek mainland, we learn that the idea of immortal Gods—forever alive, forever the same, apart from nature and human suffering—develops rather late, when society separates itself from the cyclical Goddess of death and rebirth. Zeus, the sky Father of Olympus, actually began as a seasonal vegetation God on Crete. Folklore still claims the Cretan mountain, Mt. Dikte, as Zeus's burial place. (Mt. Dikte is the horned mountain that stands so powerfully by the palace of Mallia.)

The visible body includes the Sun and the Moon and the stars as expressions of physical existence. It includes also the mythic imagination that gives life and meaning to these physical facts. When a child asks, "Where do babies come from?" the child is not inquiring about the mechanics of sexual intercourse. Our nervousness on this subject leads us to talk about biological reproduction and "a mommy and a daddy loving each other," which perhaps satisfies the child, who at least has received an answer. The question, however, touches the basic mystery of life. Where *do* babies come from? How does an individual being emerge from the invisible world to form itself around a body?

Sexuality is visible, and yet it opens us to the invisible body of desire. How can a touch on the lips or the breast or the shoulder produce a reaction in a part of the body not touched at all, the genitals? And what of the response in our bodies when we see, without touching, someone beautiful or "sexy"— a lover or a total stranger or simply a photograph? And what of the fantasies that do not exist physically in the world at all, but only in our minds? To say that sexuality exists in the brain simply begs the question. As with the origin of babies, the mystery of desire is not answered with descriptions of biological functioning.

The reality of the world (seemingly) beyond our personal bodies also leads us to the invisible. The very power of the land lies partly in our dependence on it for life and partly in the sense that something greater than we can see lives within and gives meaning to the world of the senses.

Works of the imagination make visible the invisible body. The Neolithic was a time given to great monuments. Silbury Hill in England; the giant passage mounds of Newgrange, Knowth, and Dowth; and Cahokia Plain in Illinois (whose "Monk's Mound" is the largest prehistoric earthen construction in the world, covering fourteen acres) all act, among their other functions (Cahokia Plain may have been an astronomical observatory), to make visible a human sense of the cosmos as ordered, meaningful, and alive.

Various researchers have suggested that the early pyramids and ziggurats were made in imitation of mountains. A mound is a much more direct creation. The actual interior passage in Newgrange or Knowth is a very small portion of the huge construction. But so are the cave sanctuaries in the actual mountains where the people of such places as Crete went to worship the Goddess. We should not assume that the practices and beliefs of one culture will be the same as another. Still, just as the Maltese temples may have outlined the image of a woman, so a mound or hill may have suggested the Goddess's body, especially her pregnant belly.

As well as stone circles and mounds, prehistoric people in different lands (and times) were given to giant sculptures. The Serpent Mound earthwork in Ohio runs a quarter of a mile from the tip of the tail to the mouth. A similar sculpture by Loch Nell in Scotland runs three hundred feet and reaches as high as twenty feet. Both have tails pointing west, and each originally had an altar looking east, to the rising Sun. In both cases, as in other such works, the shape of the land at that place suggested the form of a serpent. Nevertheless, this form existed only in the invisible junction of landscape and imagination until the builders set to bring it into permanent visibility.

The junction of the visible and the invisible opens the way for all art, not just giant monuments. Almost every artist has expressed the sense of being an agent for the work to create itself. We speak of the "medium" of a work of art, meaning the substances used, such as paint or stone or print or recorded sound. The true medium is the artist, who opens the way for whatever needs to emerge from the invisible body.

Myths and folklore too are the body of the Goddess, as are prophecy and oracles, for all of these utterances give form to an intuitive sense of sacred reality. And just as our bodies change and develop, growing and aging, shedding skin, menstruating or becoming pregnant, rising and falling with desire, so the visible body of the Goddess is not fixed or eternal but changes, evolves, gives birth, dies, and is reborn continually through the invisible body of time.

The temples at Malta, the passage mounds, Silbury Hill, the giant Serpent Mound in what is now Ohio—these too manifest the Goddess's body. And these too could come into existence only through human awareness, human effort, and a continuing human action. For the shape alone does not constitute the body of the Goddess. The shape must be observed and understood and joined in an act of awe and worship. Nor does this happen only once and remain fixed for all time. When G. R. Levy and others suggested that the temples of Malta formed giant sculptures of a woman sitting or lying down, they took the first step toward bringing that aspect of Her body into contemporary reality. When others, inspired by this idea, traveled to those temples and sought Her presence within the walls and in the dirt and stone, when they performed rituals there, or when they simply sat and contemplated the power of the Mother, they took the further step toward completing Her body at that special place.

The Goddess requires participation. And so we come to yet another aspect of the Goddess's body—personal experience. The phrase "seeing with one's own eyes" is a literal translation of the Greek word *autopsy*. In a medical autopsy, doctors dismember a dead body to investigate its parts. The Goddess is alive but was, in a sense, asleep for many centuries. This has been the period of patriarchy, in which we have been told that a Father God created the world and that civilization, if not existence itself, began some five thousand years ago, with the first patriarchal king-centered societies of the Middle East. (In the nineteenth century a certain Bishop Ussher claimed to have calculated not only the year of creation, 4004 B.C.E., but the day, 23 October, and even the hour, 9 A.M.)

Now, through the work of archaeologists, mythologists, art historians, scientists, anthropologists, philosophers, and psychologists, the fragmented pieces of the Goddess religion are being brought together. Temples have been excavated, texts translated, statues and paintings and myths catalogued and analyzed and explored. But all these places remain separate, isolated from each other and from meaning, until they are "seen," looked at with awe and respect by people seeking that abiding relationship with the living Goddess.

Unlike the dead body, which is dis-membered in an autopsy, the Goddess is a living body in fragments, and when we see the Goddess with our own eyes, when we go to Her temples or find Her in the mountains or in rituals created in our own homes, we re-member Her, restore Her to wholeness. And this act of seeing restores us to wholeness as well, for we heal the fragments of our broken lives by finding the links between our bodies and the Body of the Goddess.

There is another sense in which the Goddess is fragmented. The many myths of the universe created out of a dismembered body teach us that the Goddess is all around us, alive in all things, yet in so many pieces we do not realize we are walking and living in Her midst. When we go to Goddess sites or perform rituals, when we see with our own eyes, we bring together the isolated aspects of Her reality.

Honoring our own experiences at sacred places enables us (including those with whom we share our stories) to overcome the split between history and life. Too often we think of the Goddess as an aspect of archaeology, like an exhibit in a museum. We consider real or authentic only what we can prove historically, while anything we experience ourselves is somehow frivolous or sentimental. It is true we no longer live in the cultures that produced the great temples and stone circles or earthworks. And very often we know almost nothing about their actual beliefs and practices. But we still can give meaning to those places through our own experiences.

Spirituality does not exist only in ancient times or in books. It exists—it *emerges* into existence—through our own encounters with the sacred. Some of these encounters will take place at acknowledged sacred sites, others through our attempts to recognize the Goddess in our daily lives. When we celebrate our own sexuality as part of nature, when we link the rhythms of our lives to the Moon and the Sun, when we find our own ways to commemorate the ancient festivals, when we explore our own emotions at sacred places, when we see with our own eyes, we make the personal the spiritual.

Sometimes our encounters run the risk of sounding trivial, especially when we are used to thinking of religion as something that takes place in majestic cathedrals with robed priests intoning official liturgies. Virtually everyone who has attempted to follow a sacred path has experienced coincidences and omenlike occurrences. These are not the main substance of our abiding relationships, but they act as indicators or help along the way.

A sacred site is a place where previous generations of humans have experienced some special quality. They may have chosen to bring this out further by building a temple or stone circle or a cairn there. Or they may have visited the place over many years, using it for rituals or initiations or vision quests. If the place is prehistoric, like the caves in France and Spain, or has its earliest uses in prehistory, like Delphi in Greece, we may never know precisely why people chose this spot and not some other.

If we visit the place and try to experience that power—without assuming we will plumb the minds of the original builders—we may get a sense for ourselves of what makes a place special. A sacred place exists within its surroundings. Silbury Hill and Avebury Circle, England's largest stone circle, lie within the gentle farm country of Wilshire. The land there is rolling hills, land that has been tilled for thousands of years, so that a visitor becomes aware of the great generosity of the Earth in giving us life. And when we look at those hills after seeing the monuments, we can recognize the form of the Goddess, or her body lying within the shape of the ground.

When we go to sacred places or begin to celebrate the Goddess with others, our experiences teach us to find the sacred in the places around us. A rock formation in the hills near our home or a triple tree trunk in a park or an altar we create ourselves in our bedrooms—all these become expressions of the Goddess's body. We may come to a particular spot, in the woods or by a river, and sense a power and peacefulness. And we may wish to take some action to bring out those qualities—to make the body real.

If we accept the work of Levy, Scully, and others, the temples and stone circles began with that recognition of a special place and the desire to fulfill the potential. Today, such people as Cristina Biaggi are following this path. On a more modest scale, each one of us can help create the Goddess's body in a place special to our sense of the sacred.

Here are some suggestions for consecrating a particular place as a sacred site.

1. Paint a picture of it.
2. Photograph it.
3. Tell a story about it.
4. Do a ritual, alone or with friends.
5. Spend time there on a special day, such as a full Moon, or one of the ancient Goddess festivals.
6. Plant a seed there.
7. Take home a stone or a flower.
8. Build a temple there.

When we travel from our own country to experience sacred places in other lands, we act like bees bringing pollen from one plant to another, so that the plant species can continue to live. We bring our knowledge from one culture to another, and we take back with us experiences we can then apply to our own lives and society.

For those of us who seek to restore the Goddess—to look to Artemis or Inanna or Oya or to go from America or England to the temples of Malta—we risk importing alien spiritualities into our native lands. This problem is acute for Euro-Americans. Our "native" spirituality derives from places we have never inhabited, often never seen. What are we creating when we celebrate the Celtic festival of Beltane in North America? If we have no Greek heritage but feel a kinship with Greek or Roman Goddesses such as Artemis/Diana or Aphrodite/Venus, then we are taking Goddesses from a place alien to ourselves and bringing them to a place alien to them. On the other hand, if we seek out the indigenous traditions of the Americas and try to follow those ways, we may be attaching ourselves to a spirituality alien to our cultural upbringing.

Perhaps an answer to this dilemma lies in humility toward the various cultures and native traditions, while still trusting the truth of our own experience—what we see with our own eyes. I can accept the *personal* feeling of closeness to Artemis in the Greek mountains or at Brauron or on the tourist beach of Amnissos while still acknowledging I know very little about Greek culture, either ancient or modern, and I have not lived in those mountains, only visited them in the comforts of a hired car and hired rooms. And I can, in a sense, invite Artemis to the Hudson Valley, if I do so with respect to the Spirits who already live here. Just as bees carry pollen from plant to plant, so migratory humans carry spiritual ideas and experience from one land to another.

## Notes

1. Gertrude Rachel Levy, *The Gate of Horn* (London: Faber and Faber, 1946).
2. Paul Friedrich, *The Meaning of Aphrodite* (Chicago: University of Chicago Press, 1978).
3. Gershom Scholem, *Major Trends in Jewish Mysticism* (New York: Schoken, 1946).
4. Mimi Lobell, "Temples of the Great Goddess" (New York: Heresies, issue 5, 1976
5. Marija Gimbutas, *The Language of the Goddess* (San Francisco: Harper & Row, 1989).
6. Starhawk, version of traditional "Charge of the Star Goddess," in *The Spiral Dance* (San Francisco: Harper & Row, 1979).

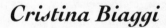

# Cristina Biaggi

# A
# Modern-Day
# Amazon

*Last spring I had a dream in which I was looking at a picture postcard from an island in the Mediterranean. Ancient Goddess bodies appeared on the landscape like sculptures, like rocks or boulders standing and lying. In my dream journal I wrote, "It's so deeply moving to see the landscape in this way, the female deified."*

*Cristina Biaggi is a sculptor who came to my attention originally through a project proposal she sent to Snake Power. Cristina and feminist architect Mimi Lobell had prepared a visionary statement proposing that a Goddess temple be built at one of the Seven Sister colleges in the east. Diagrams showed a Goddess earth mound like Silbury Hill in England and explained that it would be possible to enter this mound, like the mound at New Grange in Ireland or the*

*chambers on the Mediterranean island of Malta. Cristina wrote that she believed such a mound sculpture would be "an embodiment of the Goddess's presence and character, which forms an architectural whole with the landscape and is related to human need." She imagined the mound aligned with the Solstices and Equinoxes, with entrance stones and other features of ancient mounds and stone structures around the ancient world. And she intended the mound to be used by people for seasonal rituals and celebrations, with a symposium or lecture series connected with them.*

*Then I saw Catherine Allport's amazing photo of Cristina from their trip to Malta. Standing in the monumental doorway of the Maltese temple at Tarxien, with its endless doorways of initiation behind her, Cristina looked to me like a modern Amazon. When I mentioned this to Catherine, she told me about Cristina's Black Belt and how she got it. I asked Cristina to share her story with other women, and here it is.*

I am fifty-four years old and have been training in the Martial Arts for eighteen years. I have achieved the degree of Third Black Belt in Tae Kwon Do, a Korean Martial Art. Ever since I heard about the Martial Arts, I have been attracted to the idea of practicing some form of discipline. In fact, I am sure that if the Martial Arts had been available in the fifties when I was growing up, I would have gladly joined a school and perhaps would have gone to the Olympics.

What prompted me actually to start the Martial Arts was that I was brutally raped and almost killed in 1973. The experience left me feeling powerless, at a loss with myself and extremely vulnerable. I had to do something in order to get over the fearsome feelings, and I chose to join the Shodokan school (Japanese Martial Arts) in my neighborhood. After I had almost achieved the rank of Black Belt, the school folded, and I switched to Tae Kwon Do. I now feel much more confident about my abilities to defend myself, and I am more physically fit than ever. I think that Martial Arts are excellent for the

*Fig. 16. This carved wooden breast was made from the trunk of a fallen tree; the animals and plants of the Goddess swirl around from bottom to top, recalling the ancient Paleolithic cave paintings. Cristina calls the piece "Ziggurat," after the famous architecture in Sumer-Mesopotamia. Photo and sculpture by Cristina Biaggi.*

health, for concentration, and especially for the self confidence that women especially tend to lack.

As the oldest woman in my mixed school where I still attend regular classes, I am aware that I have become a role model for other women. I think it is important for older women to achieve proficiency in the Martial Arts, because it brings back into focus the ancient belief in the older woman as a person to be be revered, a powerful elder, a woman of wisdom and judgment. In ancient times it was the older woman who functioned as a teacher. I think it is fitting for women to practice a form of the Martial Arts because of the status of older women in ancient Oriental cultures. The older woman was the decision maker, as well as the moral and intellectual

*Fig. 17. Cristina Biaggi at a Maltese temple. The temples at Malta are some of the oldest Goddess stoneworks, dated around 3000 B.C.E., and are built in the shape of a female body. Statues of gigantic women stood within the ancient temple precincts. Photo by Catherine Allport.*

leader of her family and tribe. She was thought to embody divine wisdom which was believed to grow stronger as she aged.

Last year I decided to bring into being a dream that I have had for some time. I started Tae Kwon Do classes for women and girls in my neighborhood. I now have an exceptional group of women who have studied with me for almost a year. I started my first class by telling them about my rape and by stressing the importance for women to fight back, to take charge of their lives physically, spiritually, and emotionally. My class includes basics, self-defense, breaking boards (excellent for self-confidence), forms, and philosophy. We meet twice a week, and both my students and I feel enriched with each class, because we mutually give each other a great deal.

*UNCOILING THE SNAKE*

# Linda Johnsen

# Shaktism: The Goddess in India

*Linda Johnsen's academic specialty is India; she has written books about Indian Goddesses and women saints. In India, when* kundalini *is active and manifest, she is called Shakti and represents the untamed, ceaseless creativity that belongs to the female. A whole religion exists in India around the ecstatic worship of Shakti, her devotees going back to prepatriarchal times and extending into the present. I've noticed that in the West, nowadays at least, when people speak of Shakti, they routinely include her male counterpart, Shiva, in the same breath, speaking of the two as if they are inseparable and discussing some all-important "male-female balance." However, my own research into Shaktism suggests that Shakti functions as more of an originating and parthenogenic deity, a*

*divine totality with whom the devotee or "Shakta" (him- or her-self) unites in sacred bliss. (Another whole religion is built around the worship of Shiva and involves both male and female devotees.) Linda's work clearly focuses on Shakti as Divine Mother, in her own right.*

In our culture the Goddess has been lost for nearly two thousand years, eradicated so completely that many of us never imagined She existed. The process of rediscovering Her is so recent that when I began my research seven years ago, although *Books in Print* listed over six hundred titles under the subject heading "god," there was no entry for "Goddess."

There is one region, however, where the worship of the Goddess has survived the millennia and thrives robustly today. Ironically this is India, home of the patriarchal Aryans who contributed so grievously to the devaluation of women in Asia. Despite a hundred generations of male-dominated culture, Indian devotees still anthropomorphize the divine Shri Mata ("Holy Mother"), Rajarajeshvari ("Supreme Sovereign Empress"), Tripura Sundari ("The Absolute Beauty Transcending All Triplicities"), and Kameshvari ("Mother of Love/Desire"), just as they did over five thousand years ago when the illuminated sage Lopamudra initiated her disciples into the mysteries of Shri Vidya ("The Supreme Knowledge"—another name of the Goddess). In fact, the Devi Mahatmyam, a scripture extolling the exploits of the Goddess, is more highly regarded in much of India than the Bhagavad Gita. Hindu devotional art is as replete with images of the Goddess as of Krishna with his magic flute and coterie of girlfriends or of the glowering Shiva.

With the resurgence of interest in women's spirituality, paganism, and feminine religious archetypes, it may be of some interest to reconsider the ancient Goddess of India and the philosophical and sociological implications of Her worship. Unfortunately, the only acquaintance the average Westerner has with this spiritual tradition called Shaktism is through *Indiana Jones and the Temple of Doom*, which unapologetically depicts the devotees as drugged primitives clamoring for human sacrifice before a grotesque statue of the goddess Kali Ma. This sort of misrepresentation of any form of religion associated with the feminine principle occurred in the East as well, where Tantra (of which Shaktism is the most influential school) eventually came to be considered the lowest and "filthiest" of spiritual paths since it embraced rather than eschewed the "feminine" world of nature.

Another major reason for the historic denigration of Shaktism was its social inexclusivity. In an era when the priestly caste held a stranglehold over the religious lives of the people, reserving the more profound and efficacious spiritual teachings for itself, the great Shakta masters offered their knowledge to anyone worthy to receive it, regardless of sex or caste. Women, far from being admonished to sublimate their spiritual aspiration in service to their husbands as orthodox Vedic culture demanded, were encouraged to take up active participation in spiritual life. *Bhairavis*, female yogis, held high social status in Shakta communities. Initiation by a female guru, particularly a mother, was considered more potent than initiation by a male, for women were regarded as direct embodiments of the Mother Divine. In Shakta literature, a female saint is as likely to appear at the story's climax and save the day as a male yogi. Tales of illumined women abound. The scriptures even suggest that one must adopt the stance of a woman in order to enjoy the vision of the divine: in the Devi Bhagavatam the male gods Brahma, Vishnu, and Shiva are required to switch sexes before they are ushered into the presence of the Mother of the Universe.

Who is this Goddess? Sankhya philosophy, on which classical yoga is based, calls the feminine principle *prakriti*, equating it with the world-stuff from which each masculine *purusha*, or unit of pure consciousness, must extricate itself in order to be "liberated" from the world. In Vedanta She is called *maya*, the illusory force through which a material universe apart from spirit only appears to exist. In Shaivism She is Shakti, energy, in contradistinction to Shiva who is pure, unalloyed, and immovable consciousness; She is the active aspect of the all-embracing reality, he the static. In Shaktism, however, the feminine force is the ultimate reality itself: the paradoxical, changeless transcendent being that effortlessly and spontaneously generates the universes. In the Shakta classic, Tripura Rahasya, the sage Hemalekha describes the Goddess aptly:

> My Mother is absolutely pure and perfect. Though She is more pervasive than space itself, She is subtler than an atom. Though She is omniscient, She seems to know nothing for She is egoless. She does everything—without bestirring Herself. She is the source of all, Herself never having been produced. Everything depends on Her yet She is fully independent. Although She is formless She can be found in all forms. She is combined with everything and yet touched with nothing. Even though She is Present everywhere, no one knows Her. She is the Supreme Bliss though is not Herself limited by Bliss. Unborn Herself, She has numberless daughters, like me.[1]

"My Mother is transcendence—pure consciousness," she concludes.[2]

Though the Supreme, Radiant Being (Devi, the Goddess's most common name, means "Effulgent Reality") is utterly transcendent, She is simultaneously immanent in every atom of the universe; born from Her, it is as sacred as She.

But the Goddess is not only a vast abstraction or a pantheistic anthropomorphization. For the sake of her devotees She assumes a personal form, with long black tresses, three eyes, four bejeweled arms, and a crimson sari! The human mind cannot grasp the ultimate reality, but through the personified form of the deity the mind is given an image to catch hold of so that it can at least begin its ascent to the transpersonal reality. Devi Herself advises:

> If you are unable to meditate on my eternal and supreme form, fix your attention on my qualified form. . . . This which is infinitely changeable with time and circumstance can be grasped by the mind. Whatever form of mine your mind is capable of grasping, meditate on that.[3]

In India, the form of divinity as mother is particularly popular. "A fond mother can never fail to save her trusting child from dangerous situations. There is no doubt about it," says Hemalekha. "Bad sons are born in the world, but bad mothers, never!" said India's best-known philosopher, Shankaracharya, reassuring himself. Ramakrishna, one of the greatest Shaktas of the last century, spoke of Mother as She Who can be tethered by the rope of devotional love. The late Paramahansa Yogananda commented that although Westerners commonly worship God as Father, it is equally valid to approach God as the Divine Mother, "for the Mother is closer than the Father."

The Indian predilection for a feminine deity is sometimes denigrated in the West as an unconscious desire to "return to the womb." However, the Goddess is not always seen as so maternal or benign a figure. In fact, to Western religious sensibilities, nurtured on an unassuming, virginal Madonna—in cases where any feminine spiritual ideal has been admitted at all—the tantric images of the voluptuous Kameshvara or of the Divine Mother in Her fierce aspect, garlanded with human skulls and girdled with hacked limbs, are unmitigatedly appalling. The devotee is not here lulled to quietude in a warm, dark womb, but plunged into a fiery yoni or a gaping maw.

The Judeo-Christian tradition is uncomfortable both with sexuality and with cosmic forces, which it interprets as demonic. In the West, good and evil are strictly dichotomized. The morally ambivalent aspects of its own deity are passed over: ignoring the diabolic qualities of the biblical god who sent his chosen people to slaughter every man, woman, child, and animal in Canaan and punished them with slavery when they failed to comply—as well as the revelatory function of Lucifer, "the light bringer" who offered knowledge to Eve in the garden where she and her husband had been left in ignorance—the Western mind perceives "good" and "evil" as ceaselessly and irreconcilably at war.

The Indian Goddess, however, is so vast that She encompasses both the apparently good and the seemingly evil in Her puissant being. Swami Abhedananda writes that Indians "adorn the Mother on the one hand with evil, murder, plague, and the most horrible things, while, on the other hand, they represent Her as overflowing with blessings. . . . Among the worshippers of the Divine Mother you will find both men and women, who, in times of distress face danger bravely, and pray to Her with unflinching faith and whole-hearted love, recognizing Her grandeur and Divine Power even behind misfortune and calamity."[4]

Whether taken as a beneficent, maternal presence; a sensuous, alluring young woman; or a fierce, raging warrioress, the image of God as woman exerts enormous power over the heart. The Mother Goddess has not relaxed Her hold on the human psyche since ages immemorial, though her appearance is often covert in patriarchal cultures. In Shaktism, however, She stands in the open, inviting, seducing, daring the seeker who would penetrate Her mysteries to dissolve in Her in an irrevocable union of love and knowledge.

To effect this consummate union, consummate surrender is required. When the devotee opens fully to the vital presence of the divine, surrendering all attachment and egoism, then, Shaktas assert, one becomes a hollow funnel through which Her grace can pour. The Divinity Herself radiates through the devotee's transparent being. In *The Mother*, the well-known Indian saint Aurobindo describes this merger: "Perfection will

come when you are completely identified with the Divine
Mother and feel yourself to be no longer another and separate
being, instrument, servant or worker but truly a child and
eternal portion of her consciousness and force. . . . When this
condition is entire and her supramental energies can freely
move you, then you will be perfect in divine works: knowledge, will, action will become sure, simple, luminous, spontaneous, flawless, an outflow from the Supreme, a divine
movement in the Eternal."[5]

Thanks largely to Shankaracharya, whose Advaita
Vedanta is the most widely known Indian philosophy in the
West, the Goddess has been misunderstood and maligned for
centuries. She has been equated with *maya,* the power of delu-
sion that veils reality, whereas in Shaktism the power to veil as
well as the power to enlighten reflect merely, as the scriptures
put it, "a fraction of a fraction of a fraction" of Her majesty.
From the Shakta point of view, the world is not unreal or un-
desirable, for it is fully divine, born from and sustained by the
Divine Mother as *lila,* a form of spontaneous cosmic enter-
tainment. The point of spiritual practices is therefore not "liberation from" the world but "enlightenment in" the world; and
indeed a long tradition of tantric teachers who have not only
realized the Goddess as transcendence but have also made
their peace with Her form as the painfully evanescent face of
mundane life have shown that truly spiritual life is not necessarily world abnegating. In Shaktism sexuality, eating, working, art, indeed all vital life are not seen as evils to be
conquered or abrogated, but as *lilas* in which the awakened
devotee can consciously participate. Rites incorporating the
ritual use of lovemaking, alcohol, and meat eating are em-
ployed in some Shakta communities, although, needless to say,
these incurred the severest disapprobation of orthodox patriarchal Hindus.

One of the earliest accounts of a typically Shakta attitude
toward life occurs in the Rig Veda (ca. 4000 B.C.E.). The sage

Agastya is engaged in rigorous asceticism when his wife Lopamudra asks him to make love to her. "Virile men should go to
their wives," she teases her reluctant husband. The diehard as-
cetic at last succumbs, but Agastya learns something from this
initiation (for Lopamudra is in fact a realized yogini and
founder of spiritual lineage): that he has been wasting valuable
energy struggling against the natural urges the Goddess has
ordained. The hymn concludes that Agastya achieved both
progeny and enlightenment, having "nourished both ways" of
wordly and spiritual life, "for he was a powerful sage."[6]

Ironically, at the close of his life Shankaracharya, that
great propounder of the concept *maya*, overcome by the
majesty and mystery of the Mother, threw up his hands in de-
spair, gave up his philosophizing, and sat down to chant Her
Name. His exquisite devotional poem, "Wave of Beauty/Wave
of Bliss," begins:

> God can only create, united with the Goddess.
> Without Her, he is not even able to stir.[7]

The appeal of Goddess-centered religion was so strong
that where Shaktism did not overtly conquer, it subtly infil-
trated. Shaktism is one of the five major schools of Hindu
Tantra, but the other four as well as Jain and Buddhist
branches all eventually embraced the Goddess, usually in the
form of a "divine consort" of their chief (male) deity. As Mary
overshadows Jesus in popular Catholicism, the consort often
gave Her husband stiff competition for devotees' worship.
And where Goddess was honored, it was not so easy to disre-
gard the humanity and spiritual potential for women. The
Lakshmi Tantra, a text venerating Lakshmi as the "divine consort" of Vishnu, stipulates,

> When at the very beginning . . . I manifested myself
> in this world of systematic creation, I intentionally
> chose to assume this feminine form. (Therefore) a
> yogin, desirous of pleasing me . . . should never
> abuse a woman, either in deed, thought or speech.

*UNCOILING THE SNAKE*

I (should be regarded as) the woman(-hood) inherent in all women, that pervades the universe. He who abuses a woman thereby abuses Lakshmi (Herself).

Since woman (is) my direct embodiment, how can the yogin refrain from worshipping her? One should not commit a wicked deed involving a woman; one should not (even) think about sinful acts in connection with a woman. Those who aspire to the attainment (of fulfillment) in yoga should always act so as to please a woman. . . . [8]

Thus, even in the male dominated religions of India, the primeval Goddess continued to exert Her power for the welfare of Her daughters.

But what does this most ancient of spiritual traditions have to say to the contemporary Westerner? Perhaps the most discomfiting issue Shaktism raises is the disturbing question: Where are the illumined women now? Since the West lost the powerful archetypal figure of the Divine Mother to the patriarchal influx of Judeo-Christian and Muslim warriors over the first millennium C.E., the political status of women has sunk to the point where most Jews and Christians will not accept female priests and occasional orthodox Muslims even deny that women have souls. Somewhere in this sad shuffle the spiritual power and potential of women has been lost. Today, with rare exceptions like Shri Mataji Nirmalji Devi and the late Anandamayi Ma, most major spiritual figures are male. (To their credit, several recent important Hindu teachers have attempted to redress this balance, leaving women "dharma heirs" to continue their legacy. Ramakrishna left Sarada Devi; Paramahansa Yogananda, Daya Mata; Upasani Baba, Godavari Mataji; and the late Swami Muktananda, Chidvilasananda, as spiritual heads of their lineages. Perhaps this would have occurred in the West as well, if it had been historically acknowledged, as recently discovered Gnostic texts suggest, that it was Mary Magdalene, and not Peter, to whom Jesus passed his authority.)

For the modern woman, beset with doubts about her capacity to incarnate spiritual power, Shaktism offers the puissant figure of the heavily armed Mother Durga, mounted on a lion, charging into battle, as a potent reminder of the invincible feminine force each woman, as an incarnation of Shakti, wields. It offers examples of women sages like Vak, who in mystical identification with the Effulgent Goddess, sang ecstatically.

> I am the ruling Queen, the amasser of treasures,
> full of wisdom, first of those worthy of worship.
> In various places the divine powers have set me.
> I enter many homes and take numerous forms.

> The man who sees, who breathes, who hears words
>     spoken,
> obtains his nourishment through me alone.
> Unrecognizing me, he yet dwells in me.
> Listen, you who know! What I say is worthy of
>     belief. . . .

> At the world's summit I bring forth the Father.
> My origin is in Waters, in the ocean.
> Then I am spread through all existing worlds
> and even touch the heaven with my forehead.

> I breathe out strongly like the wind while clasping
> unto myself all worlds, all things that are.
> I tower above the earth, above the heavens,
> so mighty am I in my power and splendor![9]

Shaktism reminds us that as women and men it is our responsibility to give birth to spiritual consciousness in our lives, for the immanent is pregnant with the transcendent. And unfailingly Shaktism holds before us, now as it has from prehistory despite millennia of persecution and denigration, the awesome figure of the Goddess, the Supreme Beauty, Perfect Love, Absolute Consciousness, the Radiant Reality Herself.

## Notes

1. Rajmani Tigunait and Linda Johnsen, trans., *The Tripura Rahasya,* II, v, 108–11. Unpublished manuscript.
2. Ibid., II, viii, 26.
3. R. Ananthakrishna Sastry, trans., *Lalita Sahasranaman* (Adayar, India: Theosophical Publishing House, 1976), pp. 30–31.
4. Swami Abhedananda, *India and Her People* (Calcutta: Ramakrishna Vedanta Math, 1968), pp. 70–71.
5. Aurobindo Ghose, *The Mother* (Pondicherry, India: Sri Aurobindo Ashram, 1977), pp. 24–25.
6. Wendy O'Flaherty, trans., *The Rig Veda* (New York: Penguin Books, 1981), pp. 250–51.
7. *Saundarya Lahari,* author's translation.
8. Sanjukta Gupta, *Laksmi Tantra: A Pancaratra Text* (Leiden, Netherlands: E. J. Brill, 1972), pp. 292–93.
9. Raimundo Panikkar, ed., *The Vedic Experience: Mantramanjari* (Berkeley and Los Angeles: University of California Press, 1977), pp. 96–97.

*Gentry Görg*

# Four Prayers
# to Shakti:
# Photos and Poems

*The sensual photos and poems of Gentry Görg exemplify contemporary Shaktism — the active worship of the Goddess Shakti. These four poems are more like prayers or meditations on woman and Nature, as inextricably interconnected cells of one sacred body. Gentry is one of four sisters who, together, make up a rock band called "Goddess." Besides photography and writing, Gentry creates music, which she and her sisters perform.*

## *Poem Number One*

Sky endless

I spread my wings

To fly

Silent motionless

Desert

Of eternal dreaming mind

I am the eagle

Who glides upon the wind

I am the messenger

Of stillness

Teacher of samadhi

I am the third eye

Encompassing translucent body

I am the bird spirit

The spirit of primordial space

*Fig. 18. Photo by Gentry Görg.*

*A SNAKE POWER READER*

## *Poem Number Two*

I am the medicine stream

Flowing from the life of nature

I am the precious patchouli

The precious medicine flower

Growing in her meadow

I appear in the heart of Buddha

I am the healing golden sun

*Fig. 19. Photo by Gentry Görg.*

*A SNAKE POWER READER*

## *Poem Number Three*

Where the spring once was

It is dry

The water does not come

Will she flow

When the seasons change

As the showers return

In the winter

Does she sleep

Deep beneath a blanket

Of soil, rocks, and wind

Grass, vines, and flowers

Or have we drunk all of her

If again she climbs

Quiet and still

From her source

Within the dark

Pray thee worship

For these

Are sacred fluids

*Fig. 20. Photo by Gentry Görg.*

*A SNAKE POWER READER*

## Poem Number Four

The sun and the moon

Awaken life

Birth and renewal

The yang enters the yin

From emptiness

A seed is planted

Through a cavern of darkness

To a circle of light

A uterus becomes a womb

Of fertility

Soaked in lunar rays

And healing vibrations

A bodhisattva is born

A pure heart awakens

*Fig. 21. Photo by Gentry Görg.*

*A SNAKE POWER READER*

*Susana Valadez*

# Patterns of "Completion" in Huichol Life and Art

*Susana Valadez is, by her own definition, a "human-thropologist." Educated at UCLA, she went to live in Nayarit, the western coastal province of Mexico where the Huichols reside, and hasn't come home to live since. She married Mariano Valadez (one of the finest Huichol yarn painters) and had three children with him; now they codirect the Center for Huichol Cultural Survival in Santiago Ixcuintla, Nayarit. Susana has been instrumental in helping the Huichol people to save their traditional weaving, embroidery, and beading patterns and to continue making their traditional crafts. Besides being satisfying in itself, this work frees them from oppressive manual labor in the local tobacco plantations, the only other employment available for them in the Mexican coastal economy.*

**H**er father placed the tail of the snake into the waistband of her skirt, still alive, and held it out straight to the head. She says she counted the lines of the designs on the back of the writhing snake as one counts threads, and then wove the design. Afterwards, her father cut off the tip of the snake's tail and gave it to her to safely guard, as a power object, with her work. . . .[1]

Learning weaving designs by studying the markings of reptiles and creating meticulous embroidery and beadwork motifs based on peyote visions are some of the ways in which Huichol women produce the patterns they use in their magnificent artwork. Huichol women may undertake a traditional apprenticeship in order to excel in the arts and to acquire a huge repertoire of symbolic patterns that pertain to the divine and mythical beings. According to the Huichols, when the women go through the process of "completion" (a commitment to the deities that takes five to ten years to fulfill), the metaphysical entities who control the universe reveal their symbols and designs to them so that the women artists may use their artwork to replicate the landscape and characters of the sacred domain.

To these women, the creation of beaded latticework mandalas, the magnificently woven royal eagles, or the meticulous little embroidered blue deer are not just fancy adornments on clothing, bags, or belts, but are components of a formula, a code, which carries the cultural knowledge from time immemorial into the present. Becoming a master artist in Huichol culture is very much akin to becoming a master shaman, as the training of both is centered upon translating knowledge and information from the spirit world into the human realm. The shamans use their songs, chants, and rituals, and the artists use their patterns.

The above-mentioned woman who learned weaving designs from a snake was actually, from her point of view, com-

*UNCOILING THE SNAKE*

municating with one of the weaving goddesses who sent the serpent to act as her representative. A major prerequisite on the "path to completion" is that the supplicants acquire numerous plant and animal "allies" who communicate from the deities to the women seeking the visions. Thus each woman who wishes to complete the path of the artist must become fluent in the silent language of her allies by becoming acutely aware of the patterns and knowledge being sent to her by her supernatural mentors. In this way she discovers the real meanings of the patterns she will be "caretaking" and the secrets they contain. The allies teach the apprentices the esoteric code, a language of analogies and syllogism intelligible only to the initiated. As master artists, the women, like cultural scribes, will speak this language through their patterns.

The initiates acquire the powers and "secret language" of their animal allies by first locating them and, in the case of birds, eating the heart and keeping the tail feathers or, in the case of snakes and reptiles, cutting off the tail and sucking the blood from it, setting the animal free. The alliance between the initiates and animals must not be broken for five years, or until the initiate has encountered this animal and performed the ritual five times. If the alliance is broken before that time, the animal will cause serious harm to the initiate and her family. Once these snakes and initiates are allied, however, the initiates will possess the full powers of these animals forever. Even poisonous snakes can be picked up and held once the alliance is made.[2]

Another way the women become enlightened to this knowledge is through the use of hallucinogenic plants (particularly peyote and occasionally a flower in the Solanacae family identified as "solandra"), combined with personal sacrifice and character-building initiatory tasks the divine beings require of them. When the women have proven their intentions to their patron deities by following their

instruction, they are rewarded with a reservoir of patterns, striking color combinations, and ancient symbols. Under the direction of a variety of gods and goddesses, ancestor spirits, and other entities, their dreams become a wonderland of symbols and imagery, where panoramas of meaningful patterns take on a life of their own and communicate significant information about Huichol traditions, beliefs, and survival skills to the initiates. The patterns speak to them.

A Huichol shaman, Ulu Temay (Arrow Man), describes the technique initiates who are seeking meaningful peyote visions may use:

> Speak to the peyote with your heart, with your thoughts. And the peyote sees your heart and then you can eat as much as you want, with total confidence you eat it, without fear you eat five, ten, fifteen, twenty, it doesn't matter. And you sit there thinking, what will I see, how will it be? But in a little while you lose all of your thoughts, and then in a little while you begin to see and hear beautiful things, moving, beautiful things, and you don't move, you just sit there watching, like you are at the movies. And if you have luck you will hear things, and receive things that are invisible to others, but that god has given you to pursue your path.[3]

Anthropologist Stacy Schaefer spoke with one of her Huichol women informants, Utsima, about how the peyote visions teach the women to develop and weave designs from their heart-memory, their *iyari.*

Utsima explained to me that everyone is born with their *iyari* or receives it shortly after birth. One's *iyari* grows throughout her lifetime. Being born with the *iyari* of one's family and ancestors does not mean that the person will automatically have direct access to this knowledge. The *iyari* must be nourished in order for this heart-memory to grow. When a woman weaves with her *iyari* she does not need to copy a design. Rather, the designs she creates are a direct manifestation from deep within, from her heart, her thoughts, and her entire being. Those inspired to weave *iyari* designs learn to view nature and the world around them with a different perspective, as living designs. When they tune into this mode of seeing their world, they tap into a wealth of design sources and consciously bring their imagination into visual form.[4]

Over the years of the apprenticeship, the relationships of reciprocity the women build with their plant, animal, and spirit helpers provide them with all the knowledge and training they need in order to "nourish their *iyari*" and to fulfill themselves as women, wives, mothers, ceremonialists, and providers. They are taught such things as the kinds of offerings the deities require of them to insure good health and luck in their ventures (including luck in the sale of some of the objects they will create). They learn ways to placate the cultivation and rain goddesses for abundant crops to feed their families, and how to receive blessings and illumination from the sun and fire gods that pertain to the dry season. They learn about the many plants that will help them do such things as create their looms or dye their wool, and animals who can magically help them in all their endeavors. In short, their apprenticeship teaches them not just the mechanics of the artwork, but the mechanics of a good life and a well-rounded *iyari*.

Learning the fundamentals of backstrap weaving, complicated embroidery stitches, and laborious beading is, in and

of itself, a major feat of patience, memory, and concentration.
And the duties and obligations required of the apprentices are
grueling exercises, requiring such things as fasting, abstinence
from salt and sex, long walks to sacred shrines with difficult
access, endless hours of community service, providing and
preparing ceremonial foods, creating numerous votive art offerings, and much more. All of these ritual activities result in
a lifelong bonding between the women who undertake and
complete the apprenticeship. These high priestesses of the
artistic tradition are custodians of the goddesses who pertain
to their skills, embodying the divine essence and attributes of
their metaphysical mentors as a fulfillment of the sacred
covenant between them.

Schaefer describes some of the goddesses the artists
pledge themselves to and whose thoughts they try to emulate
while creating their artwork.

> . . . *Takutsi,* the oldest of the gods, was the first to
> learn to spin and weave. When she spun thread she
> created life in the world. By watching spiders make
> their webs she learned to weave. Another goddess
> associated with weaving is *Nivetuka,* the goddess of
> birth and weaving, who cares for the souls in the
> sky. A third goddess, *Utuanaka,* who is the earth
> mother, was the first to weave the path to the sacred
> land of peyote in *Virikuta.*[5]

Imagine the intense education that is involved for these
women who pledge themselves to study with the Creatress of
the Universe, the Mistress of Life, and the Sacred Path
Weaver! The apprentices open their hearts to the voices of the
Ancients and receive their guidance. This guidance ultimately
endows the women with the ability to use their artwork as the
lifeline of the Huichol people, because their training gives
them direct access to a storehouse of symbolic meanings encoded in the archives of the Huichol cultural memory. There is
no other way to gain access to this information in its entirety

other than going through the apprenticeship and cultivating relationships with the spirit teachers.

And just what does this cultural memory consist of, and why is it so important? For one thing, the memory contains many strategies for survival in a most inhospitable environment. These strategies are based on a profound understanding of the workings of Nature, a knowledge these mountain people have taken centuries to refine in their remote corner of the world. To those who understand the sacred symbols, the patterns function as guides for survival in the wilderness.

In the Huichol homeland everyday life is superimposed upon a background of steep slopes, forbidding cliffs, deep river valleys, and layers of eroded gorges. One of the ways they have been able to meet the challenge of survival is by patterning the natural and supernatural phenomena of their world into an orderly and predictable belief system. The patterns in the art reflect both what is visually known about the natural environment as well as the subtle unseen forces the Huichol people deal with every day in order to ensure that Nature keeps working.

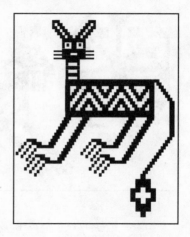

This belief system constantly acknowledges the presence and importance of patterns. "Pattern awareness" is manifested in many ways in the culture, for instance, in the constant appearance of the sacred number five, in the ceremonial circle dances, in the geometric designs in the art, in the systematic architectural layouts of homesteads and ceremonial centers (which often correspond to the solstices), in the placement of objects on altars, in the seating positions of tribal authorities, in the ceremonial chants of the shamans, and much more.

These designs are from the embroidery, beadwork, and weaving
of the Huichol Indian women. The animals and plants illus-
trated here are sacred to the Huichols, and the artwork tradition of the women holds the secret teachings shared by the tribe.
When the women seemed to be losing the traditional patterns,
having been exposed to needlework catalogues from the United
States, Susana—a pragmatist—got the idea to save their traditional patterns on graph paper, keeping them in archives for
the women when they want to "remember" them. The Huichol
women have become involved in the archival project, sharing
patterns with women from other clans and keeping the ancient
totems present in their artwork (along with the Coke bottles
and Volkswagens that they also incorporate into the work!).

*UNCOILING THE SNAKE*

Repeated patterns are evident throughout their sustenance activities, their religion, their self-governing political system, their art, music, history, and folklore.

In the Huichol culture, where for the most part people are illiterate, visual and oral symbols are the only means of expressing sacred concepts and encoding the knowledge into the consciousness of every individual. Thus the patterns in the art serve to remind not only the women apprentices but also the general populace of what is told and retold to each generation through the numerous religious-agricultural ceremonies, shaman's songs, healing rituals, and folk traditions. The information that is conveyed through the patterns in the art and other traditional means is all centered around one focal point: the undying commitment of the Huichol people to follow the primordial patterns the deities laid out for them in ancient times.

When a Huichol woman looks at the rain as it falls to the ground in the shape of an undulating serpent or as she watches her corn growing on the stalk and swaying in the wind or as she holds a peyote cactus in her hand and admires its perfectly symmetrical composition, she is seeing beyond the thing in and of itself, as she looks at it with her *iyari*. The serpent motifs that symbolize rain also signify the magic rituals she must perform in order to ensure that the rain goddesses, the owners of the serpents, will be properly petitioned to supply enough rainfall. The corn patterns she embroiders onto her child's pants not only represent the food she feeds him every day, but also the entire belief system surrounding the historical and mythological significance of the Huichol cultural transition from nomadic hunters to sedentary agriculturalists. When she weaves the beautiful kaleidoscopic peyote patterns onto her husband's belt she is remembering how she felt as she crossed the threshold into a world that was previously invisible to her but that, through the teachings of the sacred cactus, became an illuminated landscape of beauty and enlightenment.

Thus, the patterns the "completed" women artists see in nature and recreate in their votive and secular art are not just random occurrences like ripples in a pond. Rather, they are all a part of a grander scheme of things, manifestations of an invisible yet ever-present life force that responds to people's prayers when properly pampered and petitioned. The divine beings make themselves accessible to the masses through the magic of the patterns. The Huichol world works, and keeps working, because the people have never forgotten how to use the patterns as bridges between themselves and their Creators.[6]

Now more than ever, at a time when planes fly overhead and land in the once remote Huichol homeland, and many of the little girls attend new government schools rather than learning the traditional ways, it is comforting to know that many of the women's hands continue to work the patterns into the cloth. They weave the threads of the cultural memory and their *iyaris* into the fabric of everyday life, completing their destinies as caretakers of the Huichol inheritance for future generations.

## Notes

1. Stacy B. Schaefer, "Becoming a Weaver: The Woman's Path In Huichol Culture" (Ph.D., diss., University of California at Los Angeles, 1990), p. 130.
2. Susan Eger (now Susana Valadez), "Huichol Women's Art," in *Art of the Huichol Indians*, ed. K. Berrin (New York: Fine Arts Museums of San Francisco; Harry N. Abrams, 1978), p. 52.
3. Ibid., p. 46.
4. Schaefer, "Becoming a Weaver," p. 325.
5. Ibid., p. 39.
6. More information can be found on the significance of Huichol patterns in a classic study by Norwegian scholar Carl Lumholtz (etc. as written) Carl Lumholtz, "Symbolism of the Huichol Indians," *Memoirs of the American Museum of Natural History 1* (New York: American Museum of Natural History, 1900).

*UNCOILING THE SNAKE*

*Adele Getty*

# The Pattern that Connects: Healing with Sacred Plants

*Adele Getty is a ceremonialist with a powerful capacity for sacred songs; she knows more than a thousand songs by heart, many of which she "channeled" herself. She has led sacred circles for over a decade. She has trained with various Native teachers but is eclectic in her approach to ceremony and ritual. Author of* Goddess: Mother of Nature *(London: Thames & Hudson, 1991), she shares with us here a story of her personal healing, along with an overview of psychotropic plant helpers.*

In late 1979 I had a dramatic personal introduction to what the famous mycologist, Gordon Wasson, called *etheogens* (god generated within), or what are popularly known as "magic mushrooms." I was thirty years old, struggling with a very difficult Saturn return, and involved in a lovely new relationship.

My previous relationship had ended in disaster early that year. Michael* was the kind of man who walked into a room and shot sperm out of his eyes at the women present. I had ignored a dream in which my mother appeared and told me, "This man is bad news, do not let him demean you." I thought I was sophisticated enough to deal with the issues. The main issue was sexual freedom: he wanted it, and I wanted monogamy. More to the point, he was focused on the beautiful sister-friends who were my roommates. After a very stormy several months involving our entire community, we ended the affair, or so I thought.

A few months later, in June, I moved to southern California to help develop the Ojai Foundation. Before leaving northern California, I pleaded with a roommate not to get involved with this man. I specifically warned her about being lovers and the disaster of getting pregnant, which I foresaw. That summer I fell in love; Michael and my friend, who were now madly in love, visited me. Everything seemed friendly and my words were mutually forgotten as we got on with our lives.

On the Fall Equinox, while hiking out of the High Sierras, I came down with a headache and generalized sick feelings; six weeks later I thought I was dying. At the end of November I journeyed back to northern California with my partner, determined to do something about my illness. Along with the ongoing headache, sick stomach, and aches and pains, I discovered a lump in my left breast. Now I was really frightened.

My partner took me to see a physician friend of his. He examined the egg-sized tumor in my breast and asked, "What

*Editor's note: Not the man's real name.

do you intend to do if the lump is cancerous? Is surgery or chemotherapy an option for you?" My immediate response was "No!" I was clear that if I had cancer, I would treat myself through alternative medicine. He advised me at that point not even to bother getting a biopsy done, since he felt that any intrusive measures might decrease my chance of healing myself in an alternative way. I have thanked that doctor many times for giving me the chance to choose my way of living—or dying, for that matter.

The situation at home was tense. I was desperately trying to figure out how I had opened myself to this sickness. At the same time my roommate had just had an abortion, and she and Michael were deep in battle. I began asking my friends for advice, saying, "I can't find the source of this illness. Can you see what I might have been doing?" Finally one of my sisters told me that Michael was furious at me. He had been in the High Sierras backpacking, where he had experienced severe bad weather, and he thought I was the cause of the storm. He was sure I was using witchcraft against him. Suddenly things began to make some kind of a weird sense.

My first impulse was to call Michael and talk to him. He and I were scheduled to teach a class together the following week. His response on the phone was a shock. He forbade me to come to the group, even though they had invited me. Furthermore, he would not see me unless I agreed to have a mediator present; I immediately agreed.

I then had the good fortune to visit an old friend of mine who is an expert on mushrooms. He suggested that I try magic mushrooms as a cure: five grams of dried mushrooms on the first day, four grams the second day, then three grams, two, and one. Five days of mushroom eating! Considering everything else that was going on, this sounded quite sane to me, and I went about preparing for my journey.

Now, five grams of dried mushrooms is a hefty dose, and nothing can really prepare you for such an adventure. On Monday I ingested the five grams in the safety of my room, with my partner as a guide. A few hours into the experience, I found myself in the midst of a healing crisis. I literally collapsed on the floor and awoke to my partner saying, "I will be right back, I'm going to get some smudge."* During the next few minutes I began to call for my mother to come and help me. As I heard myself call out, I realized that it was not my biological mother I was needing, but rather the Earth Mother. It was almost sunset, and an ominous, swirling, misty fog was settling on the coast. To my eyes everything looked like Death coming to get me while I lay flat on my back whimpering for Mother to please help me.

It was at this moment that the history of patriarchy flashed before my eyes. In an instant I perceived how the patriarchy works to disassemble women, to knock us out of commission from doing healing work on the planet. I also had immediate compassion for Michael, realizing that he did not intend to harm me; if anything he too was a victim. I found myself thinking, "What am I doing here, lying on my back whining while Death seeps into my room?" I leaped to my feet and shook my fist at the fog outside, yelling, "I am not going to lie down and die for you Mother f—ers!" When my partner returned with the smudge, I was on my feet, livid, pacing the room, and even chuckling a bit. My life force had been restored.

An hour later when I went downstairs to get a drink, the telephone rang. It was Michael, saying, "Do we really need a mediator? Something strange has been going on. I'm not sure what it is, but let's get together on Thursday before the class and talk about it." I knew the spell had been broken.

The next day my partner and I went out to the beach, and I consumed four grams of the mushrooms. It was a glorious day, sparkling and clear. Nestled in a sand dune, I felt my energy returning, and I no longer had a headache. That

*Editor's note: *Smudge* is a word given by Native American people to a mixture of particular wild herbs that grow in North America, which have the medicinal properties of being able to cleanse and clear psychic space. Here Adele is probably speaking of sage, or a mixture of sage and cedar.

evening as we were preparing to leave, seven white trumpeter swans came flying in V formation low over the dune. For me it was a medicine sign that all would be well. By Thursday the lump in my breast had disappeared.

What is the pattern that connects? Everywhere I look I see an underlying network of relationship. All of life appears to be one web of activity, with evolution demonstrating the intricate balance of interdependent relationship. Sometimes the pattern is glaringly obvious; at other moments it's more subtle, appearing as synchronicity, accidents, prophetic dreams, or flashing insight. It is as if all of the manifest universe is a series of beads strung on the cord of some magnificent necklace. I am a bead and so are you, the military-industrial complex is another, likewise the different sexes and the races, the plants and the animals. Everything—the good, the bad, and the deadly—is part of the pattern that connects.

Unlike in the Old World, the use of mind-altering plants in the New World has an unbroken history going back thousands of years. The consumption of certain plants was and is central to the religious and healing systems of the native populations. It was not until the invention of LSD that Western botanists and anthropologists became interested in these plants and the role they play in cultural evolution. Likewise, the current interest in shamanism is directly connected to the research that has been done around psychoactive plants.

Like me, the experts in the field of cross-cultural shamanism—Peter Furst among the peyote culture of the Huichols, Michael Harner and Marlene Dobkin de Rios in the Amazon with the Ayahuasceros, Terrence and Kat McKenna with magic mushrooms, and Joan Halifax—sought out psychedelic shamanic cultures because they had already ingested a psychoactive substance. From their personal experience, they have gone on to popularize the field of shamanism.

There is a crucial distinction between the drugs promoted or banned by the pharmaceutical companies and the "teacher plants" that native peoples have used conscientiously in their ceremonies for healing and insight. One need only compare the coca plant (a relatively benign shrub that Andean native peoples have used for centuries) with its chemical derivative of cocaine, and now crack. The use of peyote by the Huichol Indians of northern Mexico is central to the story they live by, for the peyote contains their entire cosmology. The proper telling of their creation tale takes many days and is one of the most beautiful and moving stories.

In North America, the peyote ceremony of the Native American church allows Indian people to come together intertribally, speaking a common spirit language and healing what ails them; it has been particularly effective in stopping alcoholism. For years the Native American church was harassed by the government, until finally in 1978 it was given legal status, including the right to use peyote in its services. Until this time the American Indians had never been legally acknowledged as even having a religion but were simply missionized into Christianity. The Supreme Court recently ruled on a case involving an Oregon Native man who lost his job with the Indian Drug Rehabilitation Center because he belonged to the Native American Church and took peyote as part of their ceremonies. The court did approximately the same thing in this case that they have done about abortion, which is to leave it in the hands of each state to decide on particular cases. In another recent case, a white man who belongs to the Native American Church was found in possession of peyote and was prosecuted on criminal charges. The court ruled that he had the right to practice the religion of his choice and upheld his peyote use through freedom of religion.

The use of psychedelics in the New World has never been a solitary activity but one in which the entire community participates. Partaking of the teacher plants has always been a ceremonial occasion through which the people engage in healing, visions, and connection with the Spirit of Nature. The Mayan culture of Mexico has used mushrooms in their religious activities for three thousand years. The Aztec called the sacred mushrooms *teo-nanacatl,* the "flesh of the gods."

The Western history of sacred mushrooms began in 1915 when the reputable Dr. W. E. Safford presented a paper to the Botanical Society in Washington, D.C., stating that no such thing as "magic mushrooms" had ever existed. He firmly dismissed the Spanish chroniclers for mistaking the peyote cactus for a mushroom. Safford's position directly contradicted the archaeological evidence of Central America dating back before 500 B.C.E., and the Aztec and Mayan carvings of *teo-nanacatl.*

Fortunately, Safford was taken to task by Dr. Blas Pablo Reko, who declared that the mushrooms not only existed, but were still being used in the religious ceremonies of the Indians in southern Mexico. In 1938, a group of young anthropologists, including Harvard botanist Richard Evans Schultes under the guidance of Jean Bassett Johnson, attended but did not participate in an all-night mushroom ceremony with the Mazatec Indians of Oaxaca. Around the same time Dr. Valentina Pavlovna Wasson introduced her husband Gordon to mushroom collecting. The two were in the middle of writing a mushroom cookbook when in 1953, with the help of Schultes, they traveled to Oaxaca, up to the mountain village of Huatla de Jimenez, to pursue the magic mushroom. There they met the *curandera* Maria Sabina and her two daughters Apolonia and Aurora, both prospective *curanderas.* In 1955 the Wassons, along with Masha, their nineteen-year-old daughter, became the first known whites to partake of the "flesh of the gods."

On 13 May 1957 *Life* magazine published an article making it known to the general public that mind-altering mushrooms did indeed exist and that Indian shamans were still performing ancient healing rites tracing back to the Mayans and Aztecs. By this time Wasson had been in contact with Albert Hofmann, a scientist in Switzerland, and in 1958 Hofmann and his fellow chemists at the Sandoz Laboratory succeeded in synthesizing *psilocybin,* the active chemical in the magic mushroom.

In 1958 the Wassons returned to Huatla for another mushroom ceremony. This time they took tape recorders and camera to record Maria Sabina in action. On the night of 12–13 July, they participated in a historical moment chronicled in Wasson's book, *Maria Sabina and Her Mazatec Mushroom Velada*. The book contains the transcript of the ceremony and tapes of the actual event. Never before or since has a shamanic ceremony been presented to the world in such completeness. What is recorded is startling and provocative. The *Velada* or "night vigil" is an all-night ceremony where the *curandera* asks the mushroom to reveal what is wrong with the patient, whether the person can be healed, and how to go about doing the healing. The *Velada* is accompanied by smudging, chanting, drumming, and shamanic healing. In this particular case, Maria attempted to suck the illness out of the body of Perfeto Jose Garcia. He was seventeen years old and had been ill for several months, ever since working in the hot lowlands of Oaxaca. During the course of the night, the mushrooms spoke through Maria Sabina.

The ceremony began with humming, and then the *curandera* spoke in tongues. At a certain moment the mushrooms announced through Maria that the boy had had a "blow of fortune": a mountain lion had eaten his animal totem. Because his animal familiar had been killed the boy would die. At this pronouncement Perfeto collapsed, everyone became alarmed, and the other *curanderas* present attempted to comfort him. He eventually asked Maria Sabina if what he heard was true. She responded by saying yes while Perfeto moaned despairingly. Maria tried to cheer the boy up by saying that the mushrooms are clowns, as she audibly "sucked" at the illness. Maria told the boy, "Cheer up, cheer up, cheer up, don't be concerned. Look at the world. The world is pretty." At certain moments in the ceremony, she repeated various litanies that can be traced back to classical times of the Maya and Aztec. These phrases were not Maria speaking but the mushrooms themselves making the pronouncements. Here are but a few of many phrases she uttered:

> Eagle woman am I,
> Woman of the hunting dog am I,
> Woman of clean spirit am I,
> Woman of good spirit am I,
> Woman drummer am I,
> Woman who thunders am I,
> Woman of the principal Star am I,
> Music woman am I,
> Woman with "balls" am I,
> Whirling woman of the whirlwind am I,
> Woman Chief of thousands of little children am I,
> Woman of the holy clown am I,
> Woman born thus am I,
> Woman who came into the world thus am I.

Unfortunately, in spite of the efforts by Maria and the other *curanderas* present to ease Perfeto's pain, several weeks after the ceremony he died.

The recording of this ceremony is always discussed in terms of its anthropological importance but never in terms of its content. When listening to the tapes and reading the transcripts for the first time I was shocked by what seemed to be a death sentence given by Maria Sabina. She had offended my New Age sensibilities. I now understand that the shamanic world is not the New Age World, although they may overlap. I have on occasion heard of people who have consulted a psychic and were given some warning or portent of death. This is thought to be very bad form. Somehow the unspoken ethic of our time is that an oracle should always be positive, filled with light, and life-affirming. In other words we prefer to censor the oracle if it carries a negative view.

The traditional shamanic world does not function in this way, for the shaman opens herself up to the powers that be.

The cultural reality of the people is essential in understanding the oracle. The taboos that may have been broken, the spirits that were offended, the jealousy of another member of the community all must be given serious attention and appeased if at all possible. Only then will the person recover. Because shamans are expected to travel into the spirit world and view the situation in its cosmological entirety, they place themselves in danger. The power that the shaman holds is double-edged. Anyone who has spent any length of time in a shamanic culture knows that shamans are both respected and feared. Shaman wars, the throwing of medicine, or shooting of psychic darts are all part of this traditional world.

In the case of Maria Sabina and Perfeto I believe that it was in fact the mushrooms speaking through Maria. Together the people present ate the Divine Mushrooms in order to meet what was ailing Perfeto. Maria as a *curandera-healer* fulfilled her obligations as a shaman who works under the guidance of the magic mushrooms. She could not retract what the mushrooms had said, or lie to Perfeto. In the end she could only say that there was nothing more to be done for the boy.

The most fascinating and powerful of all the known psychedelic substances is a drink commonly called *yage, caapi,* or *ayahuasca,* translated as "vine of the soul" or "vine of the dead." The vine *Banisteriopsis* is found throughout the Amazon region and is widely used by the native population. A concoction is prepared from a mixture of *Banisteriopsis* and one or two other plants that become active only when brewed together. Considering there are eighty thousand species of plants in the area, the native skill in choosing the few that combine to become the "vine of the soul" is a wonderful mystery. The Indians say *ayahuasca* reveals the real world and that what we call reality is actually a dream. Furthermore, some shamans can brew the drink in such a way as to create visions of a specific color.

The *ayahuasca,* at one time called "telepathine" by researchers, is particularly telepathic and seems to have the heart of the Amazon coded into it. Reports of Westerners taking the drink began as early as 1858 and continue up to the present day. Anthropologists have studied numerous groups of people who use the *ayahuasca*. Some of the common themes of the drink were recorded by Michael Harner in *Hallucinogens and Shamanism*. The Indians describe the *ayahuasca* experience as "going on a trip," leaving the body and having the sensation of flight. Harner himself reports that during his fieldwork he drank the brew and found himself for several hours in a world with bird-headed people, dragons, and eagles who carried him to the far reaches of the galaxy, explaining to him that they were the "true lords of the universe." On his return, he told the shaman of his adventure with the "lords of the universe" and the shaman replied, "Those guys are always saying that!" Visions of huge snakes, jaguars, and dark-skinned people are perhaps the most common motifs. When Claudio Naranjo administered *ayahuasca* in an urban setting to Westerners, snakes and jaguars were the major themes. Among the Indians, these animals appear to represent their fears, which if overcome transform into songs and power. The *ayahuasca* has also proven itself useful in aiding the Indians in their hunting activities. *Ayahuasca* provides firsthand contact with supernatural beings, allowing the shaman to see the cause of illness or death by witnessing the supernatural aspects of Nature with its demons and allies. The ally spirits are used by the shaman to suck out the illness brought by the demons. Visions of traveling to distant places are common. My favorite story was reported by Roessner in 1946 while living among a tribe on the Ucayali River of eastern Peru: "While drinking *ayahuasca*, they propose that they all see something of the same subject, for example: 'let's see cities!' It so happens that the Indians have asked white men what those strange things (*aparatos*) are which run so swiftly along the street: they had seen automobiles, which, of course, they were not acquainted with."

The visions induced by *ayahuasca* are so bright that Shapibo Indians who had seen motion pictures reported to Harner that *ayahuasca* is similar. Harner agreed, and anyone who has drunk a large glass of the substance can tell you that raging visions occur whether your eyes are open or closed.

At the present moment, the use of *ayahuasca* has been spreading into urban centers and is being incorporated into Christian ceremonies, not unlike the use of peyote in the Native American church. The movement, which includes people from all walks of life, is called *Vegetalismo* in Brazil. It is not illegal, and the official view is that it is not harmful to people and may actually be beneficial. It does not make people violent but rather creates a benign presence. Like the *Velada* of Maria Sabina, the ceremony is held in the dark, with chanting, soft rattles, and healing as part of the format. Each of the participants is given a portion of the drink, the quantity determined by the shaman. The mixture begins to take effect after about twenty minutes. Compared to other known substances the *ayahuasca* can only be described as extraordinary.

The cultural significance of *ayahuasca* is extremely important. Its attempts to revitalize the human communities of the Amazon basin may, in fact, help to save the remaining rain forest. The connection the people experience with the spirit of Nature, the animals, and particularly the large snakes and jaguars who figure so prominently in their creation stories cannot be dismissed. Its ritual importance in a time when the ceremonial culture is being destroyed may be the saving grace of the Amazon and her diverse peoples—a beautiful statement of the pattern that connects.

## References

Dobkin de Rios, Marlene. *Hallucinogens: Cross-Cultural Perspectives.* Albuquerque: University of New Mexico Press, 1984.

Harner, Michael, ed. *Hallucinogens and Shamanism.* New York: Oxford University Press, 1973.

Hofmann, Albert. *LSD, My Problem Child: Reflections on Sacred Drugs, Mysticism, and Science.* New York: McGraw-Hill, 1980.

Riedlinger, Thomas J., ed. *The Sacred Mushroom Seeker: Essays for R. Gordon Wasson.* Portland: Dioscorides Press, 1990.

Roessner, Tomás. *El Ayawasca Planta Magica del Amazones,* Geographica Americana, Buenos Aires.

Wasson, R. Gordon. *The Wondrous Mushroom: Mycolatry in Mesoamerica.* New York: McGraw-Hill, 1980.

Wasson, R. Gordon, et al., *Maria Sabina and Her Mazatec Mushroom Velada.* New York: Harcourt Brace Jovanovich, 1974.

*Gloria Feman Orenstein*

# Synchronicity and the Shaman of Samiland

*An energy is awakening now to which Western women are responding. This awakening of the shamanic healing energies, combined with a remembering of the Goddess and her ancient ways, is exactly what we need to return to appropriate connectedness with the Earth, and modern women are playing a part in this important paradigm shift. Like cells in the body of the Earth Mother, we are seeing her need, feeling her pain, hearing her call, sensing her message, and speaking her truths.*

*Gloria Feman Orenstein teaches at the University of Southern California and is the author of* The Reflowering of the Goddess *(New York: Pergamon Press, 1990) and coeditor of* Reweaving the World: The Emergence of EcoFeminism *(San*

*Francisco: Sierra Club Books, 1990). In the seventies she was co-creator of the Woman's Salon for Literature in New York, which lasted for ten years, and was held at Westbeth. She has published widely, and is known for her writings on the women of surrealism.*

*Most recently she was one of two students in the world of Sami (Lapp) Shaman, Ellen Maret Gaup-Dunfjeld, from Samiland (Lapland), northern Norway, near the North Pole. She studied with her for four and a half years, until her teacher died in May 1991. The story she shares here of her meeting with Sami (Lapp) Shaman Ellen Maret and their subsequent relationship as teacher and student demonstrates clearly that the shaman calling is neither random nor limited to tribal cultures. Its universal characteristics can manifest in any time and place where healing is needed, and any one of us might be tapped with an ability to relate to the invisible, fully animated realm of shamanism.*

I was born on 8 March 1938. Labor was induced very early so that my mother (who had toxemia and pre-eclampsia) and I could both survive. I weighed in at three pounds and was placed in an incubator for six weeks. To the astonishment of everyone, and to the credit of my pediatrician, I lived. There was no Shaman, Astrologer, or Medium present at my birth who could have divined my destiny. Only medical doctors were on hand to explain to my parents why their three-pound, almost two-month-premature baby girl had to spend the first six weeks of her life in an incubator. What is even more unusual is that the incubator had virtually just been invented. Had I been born a year earlier, I would not have lived.

Stories can be told in different ways according to the information one has available with which to interpret events and according to the metaphysical perspective from which those events are perceived. The story of my birth could be given a psychological interpretation, and I could talk at length (as I have in some therapy sessions) about how fragile I have al-

*UNCOILING THE SNAKE*

ways felt and how my life always seems precarious to me. Or one could focus on the history of the technological improvements in the management of childbirth, stressing the fact that I was saved by the invention of the incubator. One might even cite the fact that I was born on International Women's Day in order to highlight the fact that I have become a professor of women's studies. Thus a single event such as my birth can be analyzed psychologically, historically, or prophetically. Each interpretation is valid, and life histories can be cycled and recycled tales, events related to each other in different ways.

But since we do not have a Shaman in our culture, no one was present at the time of my birth to interpret the karmic patterns influencing my life or to provide knowledge of my past lives or to speak about reincarnation. There was no mediator-between-the-worlds to help my parents through the rite of passage in which their child's life hovered between life and death for many weeks. Yet in other cultures, Shamans attend a birth, often perform the delivery, and then do a divination about the destiny of the child.

I want to elucidate the way in which the most ordinary occurrences in our everyday lives, in what we mistakenly think of as nonsacred reality, are really significant signposts on a path whose underlying pattern has been set in motion with our birth or, more likely perhaps, even before our physical birth into this dimension. These patterns of synchronicity, manifesting as signs, symbols, and omens, have convinced me existentially (as opposed to theoretically) that this world is sacred reality. By calling sacred the events in the material world, I am challenging the dualistic and hierarchical thinking of patriarchy that proclaims spirit to be superior to matter.

I will use the storytelling format to illustrate the patterns of synchronicity and magical "out of the blue" happenings that now, from the perspective of having been one of the only two students of the last Shaman of Samiland (Lapland, northern Norway), I understand were part of the underlying pattern of a larger spiritual calling. These magical events were one phase of my calling to shamanism and one of several manifestations that my spiritual path has taken thus far.

My Shaman teacher always said that we white Western-ers live in "the square," but that indigenous peoples and Shamans live in "the circle." By "the circle" she meant the way in which everything flows in cycles and concentric circles, the way in which everything is ultimately interconnected and in-terwoven with everything else, both across space and through-out time. According to her, there is no space and no time in sacred reality, and this is sacred reality. When I speak of "everything" here, I include things invisible to us, things not apparent in the phenomenal world. For those things that are interconnected across space and time, such as events, people, and places, are also intimately intertwined with spiritual enti-ties, events, and realities that are invisible to us, and yet very real. These spiritual entities and energies, moreover, *have real power in the phenomenal world.*

My mother's maiden name was Appel (in French it means "the call"), and my father was a drummer until he was married, which was not until the age of thirty-eight. Since Shamans are usually "called" and use drumming to induce trance, I now realize that the very nomenclature surrounding my birth might be interpreted to have been announcing a shamanic training for me at some future time. But, of course, my family and I were oblivious to this. The numbers 3/8/38 were also to become important in my life. My childhood ad-dress was 138 51 Hoover Avenue, I was married on 8/3/58, and I ultimately visited the sacred site of the Sami, Falcon-stone, near the North Pole, on 8/3/89. March 8 (3/8) is also In-ternational Women's Day, but I had become a feminist scholar and activist before I became aware of the significance of my birthday. The date I saw my mother alive for the last time was 8/30/83. I only noticed this as I read the digital calendar in the taxi that brought me home from the hospital where she lay dying. Thus, our connection in this world had been from 3/8/38 to 8/30/83.

When my first daughter was born, in November 1961, my parents were in Israel. My mother flew to the States to be with me while my father completed some consulting work in Israel. He was standing in line at the hotel to pay his bill when the clerk asked him where his wife was. He said that his daughter had given birth and his wife had gone home to help her out. The man standing in front of my father in line turned to my father and said, "I am a pediatrician. I heard what you said, and I'm curious, was it a girl or a boy?" The two men stared at each other in astonishment. It was the pediatrician who had placed me in the incubator in 1938 and had saved my life!

Two meaningful events took place in my childhood that, unbeknownst to me, were also to be shamanic signposts along my path. One was the construction of the Scandinavian Airlines building next to the subway station where I lived in Queens, New York. I always told people to look for the SAS building so that they would know when they were near my home. Never did it occur to me that one day I'd be flying constantly on SAS to study with my Shaman teacher in Samiland (Lapland), Norway.

Another incident—one common in lives of those called to be Shamans—is the strange undiagnosed illness that I had in childhood. One day when I was about six (which I now believe might have been when my Shaman teacher was born), I went to visit a girlfriend on my block. As I rang her doorbell I was bitten on the eye by a mosquito. After that I developed a series of styes on my eyes and then boils on my body, which went on for several years. Although we consulted many doctors, no one could diagnose the cause of my condition. I was the only one to insist that this was related to the mosquito bite on my eye. To my parents this demonstrated that I was a difficult and willful child, subject to frequent tantrums. I had fixed ideas and bizarre obsessions that I insisted were true.

One of my obsessions was that I had a twin sister in a northern country and that I had to find her. When I was twelve, my parents forced me to attend a music camp in Vermont by promising me that after camp was over we could go to Montreal (where an uncle was playing in an orchestra), and I could look for my twin. Naturally, they did this to humor me, but I forced them to drive all over Montreal to find my twin. I never lived down the "fiasco" of that obsession. But, sadly, my parents were no longer alive in January 1987 when I *did actually meet the person I intuited to be my cosmic twin,* my Shaman teacher.

I can't tell the story of my Shaman without first telling about my involvement with surrealism in both my undergraduate and graduate years. As a student of comparative literature I was collecting materials for a dissertation on surrealism when I found mention of a surrealist woman playwright named Leonora Carrington living in Mexico. I could find nothing about her in any of the books available, so I wrote to her. She wondered why I was interested in a few plays she had written for her sons when she was really a major painter, and she started to send color reproductions of her paintings to me. I was astonished that an artist who seemed to be every bit as extraordinary as Max Ernst (with whom she had lived before the war broke out) was not included in the many art books on surrealism that existed at the end of the sixties. I had never heard of her because she had been written out of art history. Yet her paintings were somehow very familiar to me, as if I had seen them in a past life or in my dreams.

I wrote a dissertation chapter on her plays and mailed it to her for her comments. "You have understood absolutely nothing about me," responded Leonora. "I live on many planets and on many dimensions. It is as if you're describing an elephant, having only seen its tail." I realized immediately that I had to learn more about Leonora, but she said there was nothing written about her work and I would have to visit her in Mexico if I wanted to know more. Since I had no money for a trip to Mexico, I got a brilliant but very bizarre idea. I thought that if I were to buy a Mexican dress and put it on, then perhaps the Mexican vibrations would penetrate my brain and would illuminate me as to what her work was about.

On 6 July 1971 I bought a Mexican dress in Greenwich village, put it on, looked into the mirror, and uttered these very strange words: "If I can't go to Mexico, let Mexico come to me!" At that very moment the phone rang, and a deep voice with an English accent said, "This is Leonora Carrington. I have just arrived in New York from Mexico, and I would like to meet you." I began to shake, and I told her what I had done. When we met she greeted me with her fingers making a sign of the Horns of the Moon. "What's that?" I asked naively. "Those are the Holy Horns," she replied to a stupefied, naive Upper West Side graduate student and mother of two. "The Holy Horns. Horns of what?" I asked in my most ordinary academic voice. "The Holy Horns of Consecration," she bellowed at me, as if I must have been completely ignorant not to have known *that*. I needed more clarification. "Consecration of what?" I asked naively. "Consecration of THE GODDESS!" she boomed in a voice that shook my very ground of being. (The encounter eventually led to all my research on women reclaiming the Goddess in art and literature in our time and ultimately to my book *The Reflowering of the Goddess*.)

My discovery of Leonora Carrington's art started me thinking about the omission of women from the history of the surrealist movement and led eventually to the theoretical formulation I expressed in my article on the women of surrealism, first published in 1973 in *The Feminist Art Journal*. Now, as I look back, I see 3/8 (International Women's Day) shining through that discovery. Was it all part of a pattern set in motion at my birth? Was it astrologically determined? Was it karmically necessary? How much did it have to do with what I narrowly conceived of as my "identity" as a graduate student in comparative literature? All of that autobiography now seems to be an extremely narrow way of speaking about this discovery. Did I, in fact, choose my path, or was it chosen for me? Is the scenario of our lives totally our own creation? Or are there other forces at work overruling our decisions in order to jolt us onto the path of our destiny?

*Fig. 26. Yellow-Eyed Snake Goddess. Sculpture by Mary Fuller. The carved concrete sculptures that Mary Fuller creates in northern California are delightful public works, commissioned by cities and schools for the yard and park. Like so many creative women, she has invented her own form: she mixes vermiculite, cement, and water, lets it sit overnight, and then carves it with a knife in the morning. Besides sculpting, she has published several mystery novels and writes art criticism. These are just a few of her Goddesses. Photo by Mary Fuller.*

*UNCOILING THE SNAKE*

The next summer (1972), when I went to visit her in Mexico, Leonora gave me the manuscript of her novel, *The Hearing Trumpet* (San Francisco: City Lights Books, 1985), to read. When I came to the last line of the story, I was again brought to my knees, for it said, "If the old woman can't go to Lapland, then Lapland must come to the old woman." It was a sentence that echoed the statement I had made that previous summer about going to Mexico, when I had put on my magical Mexican dress and Leonora had appeared in New York.

I ran downstairs to tell Leonora about the magic, and I asked her why her protagonist, a ninety-two-year-old woman in an old age home in Mexico, yearned so to go to Lapland. She roared at me what seemed to her to be the most obvious truth: "It's simply because the Shamans of Lapland just happen to be the most magical people on Earth, Gloria!" I did not know what a Shaman was, nor did I have any precise idea where Lapland was, but I knew that I had to remember that information forever.

For fifteen years that sentence stayed with me. During that time I curated a women's art show at the Women's Building in Los Angeles entitled "Artist as Shaman" and wrote about various visionary women artists and writers as Shamans. I was always using the word *shaman* but strictly as a metaphor. During those fifteen years, I also taught literature and women's studies at Douglass College (of Rutgers University). One day they informed me that if I wanted to keep the job, I would have to teach their folklore course. I had never studied folklore, but I needed the job, so I consented to study it. Every year for seven years I taught folklore to an audience of over one hundred students. I stressed the ethics of fieldwork, and whenever I came down from the stage having lectured about fieldwork, I would chuckle to myself: "Here I am lecturing about fieldwork, and I have never even been in the field!"

The universal intelligence is always at work in our lives in subtle ways, preparing us for our callings "when the time is right," as my Shaman teacher would have said. It took me forty-nine years to get to Samiland.*

In January 1987 I was teaching at the University of Southern California when the Shaman of Samiland came into my life. I was sitting in my office when I received a phone call from Professor Berit Ås, who had founded the Feminist University located outside of Oslo, Norway. I had met Berit, a political scientist, at several women's studies meetings I had attended. Her Feminist University had impressed me, and I had given her a small donation to get my name on her mailing list. She was in the United States on a fund-raising tour and was coming to Los Angeles at the end of the week. She asked me if she could stay with me. I told her that I had a very small apartment but that she could definitely stay with one of my colleagues who had a large house. "No!" she insisted. "We want to stay with you, Gloria." I tried to tell her that my apartment was too small and that she could be much more comfortable in a larger home. *"No, we must stay with you, Gloria!"* I was not getting through to her, I could tell. "We are coming to a little town called Glendale. We can stay with you and take a bus to Glendale," she went on, obviously ignorant of the lack of public transportation in Los Angeles. "Have you heard of Glendale?" she asked.

How could I tell a political scientist, a woman who had been in the Norwegian Parliament and in the United Nations, that I visited Glendale regularly to study psychic healing at the Healing Light Center with the chakra specialist, medium, and famous trance channeler, Rosalyn Bruyere? "You see, Gloria," Berit said, "we are coming to take a course in Egyptian healing with Rosalyn Bruyere at the Glendale Healing Light Center." I was astounded. "Look, Berit," I replied, "this is totally amazing! You see, I too study at the Healing Light Center in Glendale. And since you really can't take the bus there, not in L.A.,

---

*Editor's note: Like Machi Clarita (p. 65), Gloria Orenstein was called to the shamanic vocation at age forty-nine, the astrological Chiron return marking a person's transition to the status of elder.

I will be able to drive you there. But I still think you would be more comfortable in a colleague's home." "No, Gloria. We want to stay with *you!*" At that point she asked me if I didn't want to know with whom she was traveling. I suspected her companion was forcing the issue. "I am traveling with a Shaman from Lapland!" came her incredible reply. I breathed deeply. "Well then, Berit," I mumbled, "I guess you were sent to stay with me." And wondering to myself who else could put together the Feminist University, the Healing Light Center, and a Shaman from Lapland, I offered, "I would like to give a reception for you and your Shaman friend when you arrive."

One week later Berit Ås and her friend, the Shaman of Samiland, entered my office at the University. The cosmos was communicating a message, for I was wearing a magical dress that day that confirmed the Shaman phenomenon that I call a "cosmic twinship," a phenomenon that the Shaman had probably always known through her visits to me in the spirit world. My two-piece outfit, imported from India, was printed with an unusual pink pattern. It turned out that she had the same outfit in yellow, but not until a year and a half later did she wear it in my presence. "No way!" I exclaimed in awe, when I saw her yellow dress, knowing that she had seen we were "twins" on the day that she entered my office. "Why didn't you tell me?" Her reply was that it was important for me to make these discoveries for myself, and that her method of teaching was not to explain anything. Of course, when I first set eyes on her, and whenever she came near me, I had the distinct impression that my long-lost twin (the one I had forced my parents to look for in Montreal) had at last been restored to me.

Ellen Maret Gaup-Dunfjeld was the daughter of the Great Shaman of Samiland (Lapland—including Norway, Sweden, Finland, and Russia above the Arctic circle). In Samiland, the office of Shaman is not split between political and spiritual leadership. This Shaman of forty-four years of age had already led her people on a sit-in at the Norwegian Parliament to protest the hydroelectric plant that was being erected

*Fig. 27. Argand Totem. Sculpture by Mary Fuller. Photo by Mary Fuller.*

*UNCOILING THE SNAKE*

*Fig. 28. Leda and Friend. Sculpture by Mary Fuller. Photo by Mary Fuller.*

*A SNAKE POWER READER*

over their salmon river, the Alta-Kautokeino River. During the sit-in, women who had never left their reindeer ranches before spent the night in Parliament, and they used their dreams to prophesy their political agenda. They dreamed of flying over Rome, so they asked for an audience with the pope, which they obtained. They did this in order to publicize their cause. Then they dreamed of flying to the United Nations in New York, so their Shaman/Leader took their case to U.N. headquarters in New York. Although the Sami lost the case and the hydroelectric plant was installed over their river, the Alta case has now gone down in history, setting a precedent about the rights of indigenous peoples to their lands and waters.

When I first met my Shaman teacher, she told me she had always known of her own destiny. She came from a shamanic lineage, and her father, the Great Shaman, was always looking for signs to show him which of his children would succeed him as a Shaman. When early in life she showed an ability to do powerful healings, it was acknowledged that she would be the next Shaman. Then when an Owl appeared to her and began to talk to her about the spirit world, she was not sent to a psychiatrist (as might have happened in the West) but was given a training that lasted thirty-five years before she was permitted to heal anyone outside of her extended family.

At the time that I met her, in January 1987, one of her two sons had already died (at the age of eighteen). Two years later, her other son was murdered (at the age of twenty-four). I was shattered by this news and sent her many cassettes to console her on the death of her sons. Suddenly she called me one night and told me that she appreciated my letters of consolation, but she wanted me to know that it had been divined at their births that her sons would die young. Indeed, the Shaman's grandmother divined that Lasse, the twenty-four-year-old, would die by drowning; he had been found in a river. I was dumbfounded upon hearing all of this. I asked her if she had believed those divinations, and she replied that of course she did. Divinations that Shamans made in her culture usually came to pass, and she had no reason to doubt that these would as well. This was the hardest test she had to pass—living with that knowledge and raising her sons.

Sami diviners read omens of many kinds and see into the spirit world; speaking with spirits, with Gods and Goddesses (the Sami religion has seven Gods and eight Goddesses) and ancestors, and doing past, present, and future life readings. Since I am not a fully developed Shaman, at present I can only begin to read the language of the spirit world in the signs that surround events and in the "landmarks" that seem to underline specific things that might become important later on in someone's life. In my case, I can only read backward, and see things in retrospect—with hindsight. To some this might appear to be unfair, or cheating, because it only proves what has already come to pass and doesn't deal with other omens that I might be omitting in order to tell *this* story. I am aware of the objections to reading events in this way, but in doing even this, I know I am looking in a new way.

Later that night at three in the morning, the Shaman knocked on my bedroom door and said, "The Great Spirit told me that you were awake. The Great Spirit would like me to give you a healing now. Are you awake? Would you like a healing?" Of course I was awake. Of course I wanted a healing. Never did I imagine I would not sleep for the next three weeks! During this healing I realized that this young Sami Shaman was channeling a force that I then referred to as "the Thunder God Thor," but one that she simply called the "Great Spirit." The next morning at breakfast she said, "Gloria, I would like you to visit me in Samiland next summer." "Of course, I'd like to visit you," I replied, "and, in fact, I can come, because I'll be going to a women's studies conference in Dublin in July, and since I have a sabbatical next year, I will come to Samiland. But I must bring Leonora Carrington with me. After all, she is the one who said, 'The Shamans of Lapland are the most magical people on Earth.'" "No, Gloria. You have to do this alone," the Shaman responded. "You see, we have to walk twenty-five miles in nature, put up a tent, and go fishing." I, addicted to taxis, was immediately put off and tried to slither away from her meaning. "Who is *we?*" I asked naively. "*We* is my father, the Great Shaman; me, the Little Shaman; and you, Gloria," the Shaman snapped. "Let's not put your father to this trouble," I offered, with compassion for him. "It's no trouble for my father. He does this all the time," she responded. "Nonetheless, I can just visit him in his living room. Forget the twenty-five miles in nature, the tent, and the fishing. I'll just come and visit you and your father at home." "I'm afraid that is not possible." She was adamant. "You see, Gloria, the Great Spirit has called *you,* and we have to put you on a mountain for twenty-four hours in order for you to meet the Great Spirit." I was disarmed. Although none of this made sense to me, it was, at the same time, totally self-evident.

When I made my first trip to Samiland and found myself in the tent on top of the mountain with my Shaman teacher, who was talking to me about her work as a graduate student in folklore, it suddenly came to me. "Oh, I see it all now. I was trained for seven years to make this journey with you. Now, at long last, I am *in the field!*" All the work I had done learning about how to relate to the people one would be living with "in the field" had now come to fruition. The universe had prepared me to relate to the Sami and to be a student of a Sami Shaman, doing it with a sense of ethical responsibility toward the indigenous people who were receiving me. It had also educated me to understand just how precious my experience was and to know that I had to keep accurate journals and records of everything I learned "in the field." Had I never studied or taught folklore, I think I would have lived through my experience without ever taking notes on it, just as I had lived through my many trips to foreign countries—completely oblivious to the important lessons I was learning. And, had I not been born on 3/8 and become a feminist (out of choice? destiny?), I might never have been able to recognize the knowledge and authority of this indigenous woman who had lived the early part of her life in a tent on a mountaintop in Samiland in a family of reindeer herders. Studying and teaching folklore all those years had opened my eyes to the rich wisdom of peoples and cultures that were not a part of our very elitist, white Western tradition.

I now realize how the Shaman, my long-lost cosmic twin, had materialized out of Leonora Carrington's surrealistic novel, *The Hearing Trumpet*, which I never would have read had I not bought a magical Mexican dress and summoned her to appear in my life! I knew that I had just pulled a golden thread right through the fabric of my studies.

The nomenclature surrounding events is important. I was living on Severance Street in Los Angeles when I met the Shaman of Samiland. At the time I did not know that severance is the first stage of a vision quest. I am now living on Montana Avenue in Los Angeles. Not only does *Montana* mean "mountain," so that I have come to the top of the mountain, but I live in an apartment that she found for me via the spirit world. Since I really cannot say how the Shaman of Samiland masterminded the phone call about this apartment, precisely on Montana Avenue, I will bequeath this story to the category of "the great mystery." She simply told me she was going to do a ritual for me to find an apartment. One morning at 5:00 A.M.. I decided that I would definitely move back to New York. At 7:00 A.M. the manager of this apartment called, offering it to me, and insisting that I come see it before deciding to leave for New York. And now I am, so to speak, on top of the mountain.

In late September 1988 a strange phenomenon occurred. Mosquitoes started to die in swarms in my apartment. I could not explain this, particularly since, being an indoors person and originally from New York, I have never left the door open. Where did the mosquitoes come from? I suddenly had a bizarre idea, another of my strange convictions. I began to think the mosquitoes from Samiland (where in the summer they flood the marshland) had communicated with the mosquitoes in southern California to announce someone's death. This was by far the strangest idea I had ever entertained. But the more they died in my apartment (I was scooping up hundreds of mosquitoes each day), the more I became convinced that this was some kind of omen. This was the hot time of the year; no air was moving. It was so still in my apartment that it seemed as if all life energy had vanished. Death moved in. I called the Shaman of Samiland in Norway. I didn't want to tell her about this, but I did want to feel her energy, which was always very palpable, even across a telephone wire. She was removed and had virtually nothing to say. It was all so very strange to me; she felt so very far away and somehow unconnected.

Then on a trip to San Francisco I discovered black-and-blue marks all over my body. I was alarmed. I decided that I was probably very sick and was going to die. On the plane home I gave myself Reiki energy treatments — anything that might help before I could get to a doctor. I noticed that my hands were channeling a very powerful energy, something similar to what the Shaman of Samiland has referred to as the Great Spirit. When I got to my apartment, I found five messages on my answering machine to call Norway. It was then that I learned that the Shaman's son had died. They said he had probably been murdered. (Her younger son, Morten, had died four years earlier.) I began to tremble as I felt her grief, and I realized that the black-and-blue marks were manifestations of the spirits beating at me to inform me.

Shortly after the phone call to Norway, I heard from my friend Jillian Aronstam that Monica Sjöö, artist and author of *The Great Cosmic Mother*, had just arrived in town and was staying at Jillian's house. When I told Jillian about Ellen Maret's son's death, she invited me to come and be with her and Monica Sjöö. Monica had also lost two sons and was also from Scandinavia. There was a strange ghostly "twinship" about how these unprecedented events were aligned at the moment. I had always felt that Jillian was somehow related to me — in a cosmic way. In fact, people often called her Jillian Orenstein, and me Gloria Aronstam. Jillian performed healing rituals for me that night, and Monica tape-recorded a letter in

*UNCOILING THE SNAKE*

Swedish (which Ellen Maret understood), in which she could share her own experiences about the loss of her two sons. I also realized that the mosquitoes had probably been messengers of Death, just as I had imagined. The next summer I learned that the Norwegians have a word *ganflue*, which roughly means sending mosquitoes to shamanize someone and bring portents of a dark omen.

For example, during the summer of 1989 the Shaman of Samiland and I hiked into the mountains, and we did a ritual in which she called upon our spirit guides. Then she said, "Gloria, our guides have come in the form of mosquitoes. Can you see them? They are circling around us now." Of course there were hundreds of mosquitoes in the mountains, as there had been every summer. How could I have believed that they were our Spirit guides? Except I remembered the mosquitoes who had died in my apartment in September of 1988, and I knew that she was correct. These mosquito events intersected with physical symptoms that doctors could not explain—the styes, the boils, later the black-and-blue marks on my body. I was beginning to see the way physical ailments are manifestations of messages from the spirit world.

I tell you now that I am the Bear in the spirit world in order for you to understand the full symbolism of how the Shaman of Samiland's death in Bergen, Norway, was experienced by me and my community here in southern California.

Ellen Maret's father, the Great Shaman, gave me a Bear pin in a private ritual and named me *Guov'zza*, the Bear, an animal that is both sacred and powerful to the Sami. Endless stories could be told about my Bear pin. At one point I lost it on a two-mile walk. When I came home, devastated to find my magic pin missing, I called Norway in a panic. My Shaman teacher instructed me to do a ritual that night in which I would ask the spirits to make me into a Bear Spirit. Then she hung up the phone and I was left standing there stunned. How was I ever to do such a thing? I set my mind to inventing a ritual and worked at it for many hours. The next day I went back to Westwood to look for the pin. On the way home, as I was

*A SNAKE POWER READER*

walking uphill, I began to lumber like a Bear. I assumed that I was just feeling tired. But then I felt myself getting taller, and suddenly it occurred to me that this must be what Bear Spirit felt like. When I looked down, there was my lost Bear pin on the ground in front of me. I was thunderstruck.

During the summer of 1990, when the Shaman of Sami-land was clearly dying in her third bout with cancer (and choosing not to go to a hospital until it would be too late), I started to experience the same physical pains on the right side of my back, neck, and head, that I had suffered in 1980. These were pains that no doctor could diagnose, nor could they be eased by three years of chiropractics, acupressure, and bio-feedback. They simply lifted mysteriously one day in June 1983. Where those pains had come from was always a mystery, and what caused them was never known. Then in 1990 I realized the same pains had returned. I began to put two and two together and asked the Shaman exactly when her younger son had died. I was not surprised to hear that he had died in June 1983 and that she had been involved in a "spirit war" at that time, just as she was involved in one at the moment I asked her this question. Now I knew that my energy field had, in fact, been informed of her first son's death, even before I had ever met her or had a Shaman in my life. Indeed, it began to seem as if my life had always been connected to hers, even as far back as her birth, for she was born when I was six, and it was approximately at that age that I was bitten by the mosquito.

By early May of 1991 it became clear that the Shaman's cancer would not be cured. When she became unconscious (or when she began to take her leave of us for the spirit world), I could no longer speak to her on the phone, as I had done almost every day during the last year of her life. If I could have told her one more thing, I would have said, "Please, if you must die soon, can it be when I am with my friends at our yearly Jewish feminist spiritual retreat, on May 25th, Memorial Day, for then I will not be alone when the sad news comes. And I do so want to be with friends at that time." But I could

*UNCOILING THE SNAKE*

not say it to her. Nevertheless, she knew it all. For on May 24th, I was called for in a car driven by a woman I had not met. This woman, Ann Brenner, is a therapist who specializes in grief and mourning. Miriyam Glazer, one of my dearest friends, and Marcy Shapiro, a doctor friend from New York, were also in the car.

I began to feel as if this car were a limousine made to the specifications of my needs. On the way to the retreat center we stopped, seemingly at random, to buy flowers. I was going to create an altar to the Hebrew Goddess, Asherah, at the retreat, and I wanted to buy flowers for the altar. The florist carried mostly dried flowers, along with some lovely yellow lilies. Since they were the only fresh flowers in the shop, I took the lilies. Then the florist asked me, "Would you like some bear grass to go with the yellow lilies?" Miriyam, who had heard all my stories about being the Bear, turned to me and laughed. She said, "Only you, Gloria!" So I bought the bear grass, which, I must admit, I had never even heard of before.

We arrived at the Shalom Center (*shalom* means "peace") in the town of De Luz (meaning "light"), had dinner, talked for a while, and went to sleep at midnight. At 1:00 A.M. came the phone call announcing the death of my Shaman teacher. I was asleep, and one of the other women answered the phone. No one woke me up. Instead, they all planned a funeral ceremony. The funeral took place on the Asherah Goddess altar that I created, on May 25th at the Shalom (Peace) Center in De Luz (Light), California. It was performed by Ann Brenner, who specializes in grief and mourning. Later that day I received a phone call from a friend of the Shaman, Marina, who asked me what kind of flowers I would like to have her send from me to the funeral in Norway. I said, "Whatever is beautiful and is in bloom now." Marina responded, "Her favorite flowers have always been yellow lilies." I gasped. I had bought the yellow lilies without knowing this. And they rested in a vase with the bear grass on the Asherah Goddess altar that I created in Peace and Light on the day that she died.

*A SNAKE POWER READER*

We played a tape of the Shaman of Samiland singing *Yoiks* at the funeral service. It was clear to everyone that she had spiritually orchestrated this cosmic event. We were all in perfect alignment in space and time at that moment, which was a miracle in my life and in the life of my community. For a week preceding her death, the clouds above Montana Street seemed to be speaking to me. I saw angels and women float by overhead. I saw hearts and colors in the sunset I had never seen before. The clouds are still speaking to me.* Now I often see reindeer in the clouds. I used to wonder how the Shaman of Samiland could tell me that she did not fear Death. But, of course, I understood that she visited the spirit world many times, that she spoke with the spirits of her ancestors, and that, as she taught, "Death is always sitting on your left shoulder."

Now that she has transformed my life, I no longer look upon a mosquito as something insignificant. I also pay close attention to the names and numbers surrounding any event. I can even see the shape of events, as I connect symbols with each other across time and space. Perhaps I learned how to do this from studying fiction. I always say that literature is the best major for a potential Shaman student, because you learn to "suspend disbelief." From now on I will always be mindful of the possible consequences of any event when someone says, "Gloria, I'd like you to come visit me this summer." But most of all, there can never again be an event in my life that I do not see as already embedded in a vast web of interconnected symbols, signs, omens, and meanings. Nothing really dies. All is alive, whether visible or invisible, past, present, or future. Everything is infused with a spirit energy, even this text. I can no longer read anything in innocence.

From my perspective, all of life is like the manifestation of that yellow lily. We simply do not realize the many dimen-

*Editor's note: In Tibetan Buddhism, the Dakini is a female wisdom spirit or Goddess who manifests on the wind and in the clouds. Dakinis function as priestesses of the dead, carrying the spirit of the departed to the other side. It is the Dakini who rules synchronicity and magical phenomena.

sions of interconnections, causes, sources, the agency of visible and invisible, living and dead entities that lie behind the appearance of any phenomenon. We are completely innocent—until the spark is ignited that sets ablaze the hidden pattern, what I call the web, what the Shaman of Samiland called the "circle." In answer to Sartre, I would say that nothing is contingent, without meaning, *de trop*. On the contrary, everything is precise, exact, even karmically perfect; but we are so limited that we cannot possibly know the explanation for most things. This kind of knowledge—revealed knowledge, illuminated knowledge, gnostic knowledge—is what shamanism is about on its deepest philosophical level.

But this story is also about the Goddess—occulted, occluded, obscured, and ultimately revealed. I must close by telling you how the lost Sami Goddesses manifested in academia in order to find me.

One of the most interesting things I learned about the Sami people was that they had eight Goddesses. They have a Mother Goddess, known as *Madder/acca*, and a Triple Goddess—a Trinity composed of *Sar/acca*, *Juks/acca*, and *Yuks/acca*. Try as I might to find out about these Goddesses, I could not. No one remembered much about them; they simply occupied symbolic places in the Sami tent. You see, the Sami have been Christianized and colonized, and in this process they lost their Goddesses. Except for one thing: The Goddesses are alive in ritual. I know that because the Shaman of Samiland always invoked them when she performed rituals, and their energies would flood the room. I also learned that the same Sami Goddesses were celebrated in Solstice and Equinox rituals known as *Acca/demias*.

From this matristic perspective, there is a certain feminist logic to the way in which the Sami Goddesses visited me in academia. Naturally, this is why we speak of "the groves of Academe." They are Goddess groves. Now, whenever someone asks me if my interest in the Sami is purely academic, I smile and say, "Of course, it's completely Acca/demic!"